Our decade and our gener)k
we will see those whom we he ㅑo
exercise moral courage in the fa.. .. .pp .th
when others are choosing doubt and fear, who sacrifice time or
comfort to bless a brother or sister in need.

Those who make such choices are those who are truly great
in the sight of God.

"I am confident that there are many great, unnoticed, and
forgotten heroes among us," President Howard W. Hunter said.
"I am speaking of those of you who quietly and consistently do
the things you ought to do. I am talking about those who are
always there and always willing. I am referring to the uncommon
valor of the mother who, hour after hour, day and night, stays
with and cares for a sick child while her husband is at work or in
school. I am including those who volunteer to give blood or to
work with the elderly. I am thinking about those of you who
faithfully fulfill your priesthood and church responsibilities. . . .

"I am also talking about those who instill in others faith and
a desire to live the gospel—those who actively work to build
and mold the lives of others physically, socially, and spiritually.
I am referring to those who are honest and kind and hardwork-
ing in their daily tasks, but who are also servants of the Master
and shepherds of his sheep. . . .

"It appears to me that the kind of greatness our Father
in Heaven would have us pursue is within the grasp of all who
are within the gospel net. We have an unlimited number of
opportunities to do the many simple and minor things that will

ultimately make us great. To those who have devoted their lives to service and sacrifice for their families, for others, and for the Lord, the best counsel I can give is simply to do more of the same" ("What Is True Greatness?" *Ensign*, Sept. 1987, 70–72).

Recorded in these pages are the true stories of a few such heroes. The names of these heroes have sometimes been changed to protect their anonymity or to enable them to keep their good works secret. For the same reasons, the authors of the stories have sometimes chosen to use pseudonyms, and sometimes details have been slightly altered when the author desired to let his or her specific good works be seen of God and not of man. But the stories remain true, both in spirit and in fact, testimonies of the goodness of the men and women who surround us in our day to day lives.

I express my gratitude to those who have allowed me to include their stories in this book, including those who granted permission to use previously published material. I also am grateful to those who helped to gather, record, and type a number of these stories: Dee Ann E. Barrowes, Orlando T. Barrowes, Camille Parry, and Vicki L. Parry. Finally, I wish to thank the publishing staff at Deseret Book for their excellent and professional work. Those who made significant contributions to this work include Jana Erickson, Tonya Facemyer, Tom Hewitson, and Richard Peterson.

We believe in being honest.

ARTICLES OF FAITH 13

TRUE ... OR ... FALSE
WAYNE B. LYNN

I had stressed the need for honesty, explaining to my students that many times we don't even know our integrity is being tested. I had shared with them experiences like Mr. Larkin's at the corner drugstore. He had told me that Alfred could not be trusted.

"How do you know?" I inquired.

"Well," he said, "often when I have lots of customers and I'm the only salesperson in the store, I let young people make their own change from the cash drawer. I started coming up short, so I carefully counted out the cash before and after several youngsters had made their own change. They were all honest with me except Alfred. I gave him two chances, and he failed me both times. So now I know that Alfred can't be trusted."

"Have you told him?" I asked.

"No, I never have. I just watch him very closely. I hope he never asks me for a job or for a recommendation."

So my class should have been prepared for the snap quiz I gave them that Thursday afternoon. It was a twenty-question, true-or-false test covering material we had discussed during the week. They finished the test just as the bell rang for dismissal.

"Please pass your papers to the center of the aisle," I instructed.

Later that evening I very carefully graded each paper, recording the score in my grade book but leaving no marks on the papers.

When the class assembled the next morning, I passed the papers back and, as usual, asked that each student grade his own paper.

I read each question aloud and with a word of explanation announced the correct answer. Every answer was accompanied by the usual student groan or sigh of relief at having given a wrong or right response.

"Please count five off for each one missed and subtract the total from one hundred," I instructed. "Your scores please. John?"

"85."

"Susan?"

"95."

"Harold?"

"80."

"Arnold?"

"90."

"Mary?"

The response could hardly be heard: "45."

I went on, putting the grades in my grade book, carefully

recording each oral report next to the grade I had recorded the night before. The comparison was revealing.

A stillness settled on the class when I explained what I had done. Many did not look up from their desks; others exchanged furtive glances or quick smiles.

I spoke quietly to my students. "Some of you may wish to talk to me privately about our experience here today. I would like that.

"This was a different kind of test. This test was a test for honesty. Were you true or false? I noticed that many of you looked at Mary when she announced her score of 45. Mary, if you don't mind, would you please stand up? I want each of you to know that in my book Mary just achieved the highest score in the class. You make me feel very proud, Mary."

Mary looked up rather timidly at first, then her eyes glistened as she broke into a smile and rose to her feet. I had never seen Mary stand so tall.

"True . . . or . . . False," *New Era*, Sept. 1978, 11.

Charity suffereth long, and is kind.

1 CORINTHIANS 13:4

SINGING TO ELLIE
Patricia Ann Hart

Our home was always the one where the neighborhood kids gathered to play. We always seemed to have extras around the house. My parents were very tolerant and always said they would rather have their children at home with friends than have their children gone someplace else to play. They were especially sensitive to kids who might be left out or teased, and they stuck up for those kids.

One girl in our neighborhood was so rude and mean that no one liked to be with her. Her name was Ellie. Ellie was aggressive and had problems in school. My mother thought that all children were valuable and that Ellie needed someone to love her. She said that we should invite her for a sleepover, that it would be good for her to be in our home with us.

Well, we thought it was a terrible idea, and we said so. We complained and complained.

Mom said that if we would invite Ellie over, we could also invite a few of our other friends. Then Ellie could be with a whole group of us who were her age. We finally agreed.

At first the night seemed to go pretty well. Then everything began to fall apart. Ellie began to be pushy and bossy. When Ellie got to the point that she wouldn't even do what my mother asked, Mom decided it was time for bed. We all obediently got our sleeping bags and spread them out on the floor—except for Ellie. She wouldn't get her bag. She wouldn't settle down. All of the rest of us were in our places and Ellie was still running around. Finally my mom turned off most of the lights and just sat in a chair to see what Ellie would do. Ellie went to a far corner of the room and just sat there.

We were all so intrigued to see what would happen next that we couldn't go to sleep.

After a while my mother began to sing Primary songs. It didn't seem quite like her, but I liked it. I know Mom was exhausted after a very long day, but she sang and sang for a long time.

I don't know when it started. The most amazing thing began to happen.

I noticed that Ellie had moved a little, just barely. She had come a little way out of the corner. My mother continued to sing. As I watched, the girl moved ever so slightly. We were all so quiet, I didn't know who was asleep and who was awake. My mother sang and sang.

I don't know when I fell asleep, but it was to my mother's singing.

When I awoke the next morning Ellie was still asleep. I couldn't believe that she was so still.

After all the girls left I asked my mother what had happened. This is the story she told me. The night before when Ellie wouldn't settle down, my mother was worried. She didn't know what to do. Should she give up? Should she call Ellie's parents? She decided that she couldn't give up. She said a prayer and asked for help and the answer came. She should sing Primary songs.

She began to sing. She sang and sang and wondered why. Then she too noticed that Ellie began to move, ever so lightly.

My mother continued to sing. Ellie inched out of her corner. Mom ran out of songs and began to sing some of them over and over, but she did not stop.

Gradually, a miracle happened. As my mom sang, this rude and unloved girl crept closer and closer to her. The songs kept coming. Ellie kept moving, slowly, but surely.

My mother sang for three hours! Her voice was strained and her body depleted, but still she sang. At the end of that time Ellie was hugging my mother around her legs. Mom was afraid to move. She didn't want to disturb Ellie, so she sat still and just kept singing. When Ellie finally fell asleep, my mother gently covered her with a blanket and said a prayer of thanksgiving. Then she stayed with us the whole night.

I loved my mother's singing. But more than that I loved my mother.

Wherefore, ye must press forward with a steadfastness in Christ,
having a perfect brightness of hope, and a love of God and of all men.

2 NEPHI 31:20

WHAT WOULD THE SAVIOR DO?
ANITA R. CANFIELD

A husband and wife I'll call Jim and Martha brought hope back into their lives as they brought hope to someone else through love and service. They had been married thirty years. Their children were doing well, their financial security was established, they were enjoying life and each other, they were the best of friends. Then the devastating news came that Martha was dying. It was a slow-growing disease but an incurable one. She could expect to live two, maybe three more years. After the anger, denial, and sorrow of it all passed, they began to make plans. They would travel and visit their children and spend all their time together.

Then at a Church auxiliary meeting it came to Martha's attention that a family in their ward was in need. The husband was not active in the Church; the wife, who was not a member, had recently had a stroke and was paralyzed permanently. She was only twenty-nine years old and the couple had three small children. Their meager savings were gone, spent on hospital bills.

The husband was struggling to look after the children, maintain a job, and care for his invalid wife.

Martha went home from that meeting touched deeply by the plight of these people. For the first time since hearing of her own condition, she felt the relief of being concerned for someone else. Through a sleepless night she thought about how good her life with Jim had been, how blessed and full. This illness was a mountain for them, but they had the hope of eternal life together someday. She knew they had the resources to alleviate some suffering for this young couple. What would the Savior do? For the first time in months she felt a brightness of hope. *This is right,* she thought. She felt the Spirit moving her toward a love of God and of all men.

When morning came she told Jim of her restless night, of her promptings to help, of the hope she was feeling. She said that to travel would be nice, but after she was gone Jim would only have photographs and a few memories of that time. If they helped this family, Jim would see the fruits of their labors for years to come. She asked him if that wasn't what the gospel was all about? She could die having been productive to the end, and she said it would bring peace to everyone.

Jim could not disagree. He felt the Spirit, and he sensed renewed hope. That morning they knelt in prayer for guidance, for inspiration, for love. That evening they paid their first visit to this needy little family.

In the two years and eight months that followed they brought hope into the lives of this couple. They remodeled their living room, adding a bigger window so the mother could watch her children at play and be able to enjoy the outside. Jim and Martha bought her a special bed so she could be more comfortable by her window to the world. They worked hard planting a rose garden right in front of this window, and they also maintained the yard work. They spent countless hours tending the children and holding them, trying to comfort them as their mother no longer could. They took the children on short trips with them, to the park, on numerous picnics. They made sure they went to church every Sunday. Jim and Martha made special meals twice a week and had family home evening on Mondays with the family. It wasn't long before the father was attending church again. And soon after that his wife wanted the missionary lessons.

The stake missionaries were called in, and Jim and Martha helped make every meeting a special event. It was a joyous and emotional day when Jim helped lower this young wife and mother into the baptismal font. Tears streamed down his cheeks as he helped support her fragile body while her husband raised his hand to the square and began, "Having been commissioned of Jesus Christ . . ."

That night Martha told Jim, "These have been the best years of my life. I love the Lord, I love life, I am at peace."

Martha was too ill to attend the temple to see them sealed. But Jim reported back every detail, and when the photographs arrived she lovingly memorized each one. Martha passed away several months later.

The fast Sunday after the funeral, the young husband bore his testimony of the Savior's love in his life. He said he had seen the Savior on the faces of Jim and Martha. Love, he said, had brought back hope into his life and the lives of his family. Even the hope, he wept, of eternal life.

Not long after that his wife also died. . . .

A love of God and of all men brings a true and perfect brightness of hope, even to the end.

Canfield, *A Perfect Brightness of Hope*, 97.

*[He was] preaching the kingdom of God, . . . with
all confidence, no man forbidding him.*

SPLITS WITH ELDER BEGAY
RANDAL A. WRIGHT

Several years ago when I was serving as a stake missionary, I was privileged to meet a full-time missionary from Utah named Maurice Begay. Elder Begay was a full-blooded Indian and a perfect example of one who had "blossomed as a rose." He showed me, during a "missionary split" one night, why we sometimes need to let our lights shine, even when it's hard.

That night as we were out tracting, we drove into a poor area of town. Elder Begay asked me to pull up to a particular mobile home so we could tract it out. I tried to tell him that I was sure the people who lived there would not be interested in the Church, but he would not listen and began to walk up the driveway. I followed him past a couple of junked cars and scattered trash up to the trailer door. I was more than a little nervous as Elder Begay knocked loudly on the door. My confidence sank even more when the man of the house opened the door. He had a cigarette in his mouth, no shirt, tattoos all over his arms, and a scowl on his face. "What do you want?" he asked.

I thought, *I want to go home. What do you think I want?* But I said nothing.

Elder Begay told him who we were and asked if we could come in and share a message with his family about Christ's visit to the Americas. After a long pause, he invited us in. In his small living room sat his wife and four children. All needed a comb, a bath, a handkerchief, and some better clothing. There was tension in the air as we sat down, and it became obvious that no one was going to speak to us because of their involvement in a TV movie.

After a short time, Elder Begay told the family we had a message to share with them. No one responded to his comment. I became more nervous and had a strong desire to get up and leave. The elder tried two more times to talk with the family about the Church, but still they would not reply.

After we had sat there for about fifteen minutes, Elder Begay did something that took as much courage as anything I have ever seen. With no warning this young missionary picked up his chair and set it right in front of the TV set, then sat down so the family could not see the movie. Then he reached around and turned off the set. "You don't mind if I turn this off, do you?" he asked. There was an eery silence in the room as the family stared at him in disbelief. I have never wanted to run so bad in all my life.

After what seemed like an eternity, the man replied, "I guess not; I've already seen that movie anyway." Hearing that brought me more relief than I can describe. That night a young Lamanite missionary taught that family about Joseph Smith and the

Restoration. The family was not interested in the Church, just as I had first suspected, but I had witnessed one of the most inspirational events of my life.

From "Learning for Myself," in *High Fives and High Hopes*, 134–35.

He that is faithful in that which is least is faithful also in much.

LUKE 16:10

"I SANG A SONG TO MYSELF"
E. DALE LEBARON

In 1992, the Church was officially recognized in Tanzania. One of the first to accept the gospel there was Robert Israel Muhile. While working and studying in Cairo, Egypt, Robert attended his first Latter-day Saint church meeting on Christmas Day 1990. There he met Elder and Sister Whitecourt. He observed: "They were very kind people. I liked them so much. They made me want to change my life." After Robert was taught the missionary discussions and baptized, he said, "I felt a great joy and peace in my life."

In May 1991, after being ordained an elder, Robert returned to Tanzania so he could share the gospel with his family. However, Robert's family lived more than six hundred miles (a three-day bus ride) from the nearest branch of the Church, in Dar es Salaam, so he found himself isolated from other Church members. He wrote to the Africa Area presidency and Nairobi mission president Larry Brown to let them know that he had joined the Church. After six months without partaking of the sacrament, Robert traveled to Nairobi, Kenya, to ask President Brown if he could administer the sacrament to himself each Sunday. His request was granted. Robert said: "I know how important those emblems are. I didn't feel well spiritually. In Nairobi, I had opportunity to partake of the emblems and bear my testimony."

Back in his home village, Robert invited his family to join him for worship service each Sunday, but they chose to attend their own church. So he held his own service alone. He said: "I prepared water and bread. I also had more water to clean my hands and a small towel. I sang a song to myself out loud. I had my hymn book. After that I offered an opening prayer. Because I was alone, I didn't have any business to do, so I sang the sacrament hymn and prepared the sacrament. Then I knelt and blessed it and took it. After the sacrament I covered it, as we respect it always. I offered myself a talk—my testimony. Then I sang as we did in Sunday School and then read from *Gospel Principles*. I finished with a prayer. I then attended priesthood meeting. After singing a hymn, I said a prayer and then read a lesson from the priesthood manual. After that, I finished by singing and then offered the closing prayer. Each Sunday I had all three meetings. When I partook of the emblems it helped me to be more worthy."

Since that time Robert has married a fellow young adult convert in the Johannesburg South Africa Temple.

From E. Dale LeBaron, "Pioneers in East Africa," © by Intellectual Reserve, Inc. Previously published in the *Ensign*, Oct. 1994, 24.

The mouth of the righteous speaketh wisdom.

PSALM 37:30

"GO HOME TO YOUR MOTHER"
KAREN LARKIN

One of the joys of my childhood was that I lived in close proximity to my paternal grandparents. There were only fields between my house and theirs, and I loved to run from one house to the other. I spent many hours with my grandmother. She was my Sunday School teacher. Often on Sunday afternoons, when everyone in my house was napping, I would run over to Grandma's house. There she would be, sitting in her big chair preparing the lesson for Sunday School the next week.

She would stop and ask me if I wanted to play a game with her. Of course I would say "yes." She often asked me to sing her a song or play a little piece on the piano. As I became more proficient she would pick out pieces of music that she loved like "Beyond the Sunset" or "Galway Bay," and ask me to play them for her. She would sit in her chair with her eyes closed and listen, occasionally making a comment about the song and why she liked it or what memories it held for her. She would always tell me how talented I was.

When my grandma baked cookies she was never selfish with

them. I could have as many as I wanted. I just knew I was her favorite grandchild—though in later years I discovered that all of the grandchildren thought the same thing about themselves.

One day when I was about twelve years old, my grandmother and my mother had a misunderstanding. My mother said some things to my grandmother that were very hurtful. Grandma left my house in tears. I watched as she began to walk through the fields toward her house.

I felt terrible. I was truly hurting for my grandmother, whom I loved dearly. I ran out after her and caught her about halfway between our houses. I kept saying how sorry I was for the things my mother had said and that I loved her. Grandma took me into her arms and through her tears she said, "I love you too, dear. But you go home to your mother. She needs you."

I couldn't believe it. My grandma was crying because she had been hurt. My mother wasn't crying—she was just angry and at home complaining about what had happened. But Grandma knew it would be harmful for her to let me take sides between her and my mother. Instead of letting me comfort her, she sent me home to my mother.

It was many years before I understood how unselfish and right she had been in sending me back. But in time it became a powerful testimony to me of her strength and depth of character. The cookies were only a bonus.

Execute true judgment, and shew
mercy and compassions every man to his brother.

ZECHARIAH 7:9

"THEY'RE GOOD PEOPLE"
ORLANDO T. BARROWES

My mother, Fern Rees Barrowes, was the stake drama specialist in an era when each ward prepared and presented a thirteen-minute play called a roadshow. These were popular, and competition between wards was keen. On the first night of performances, the show literally traveled on the road, going from church building to church building so members of all the wards in the stake could see all the shows. At each building were judges who rated the different shows on various aspects of the performances. On the second night all of the performances were done in one building for all the various cast members to see.

On this second night awards were given for "Best Show," "Best Music," "Best Scenery," and so forth. The "Best Show" award was the most coveted. All of the judges' scores were added together to determine who had the highest cumulative score. That ward received the "Best Show" award.

One year one of the wards, which did have an outstanding show, did not receive the "Best Show" award when they anticipated doing so. The directors of that ward's show were hurt and upset. They were vocal about their feelings and left the building loudly complaining.

Within a couple of days my mother decided to visit those leaders and explain the point system. Perhaps she could soothe their hurt feelings. Since Mom didn't drive she took me as her chauffeur. As we drove I was free with my opinions. "Maybe it's not a good idea to go into a lion's den," I said. "They're just poor losers anyway."

I was surprised when she stood up for them. She explained that they had given a lot to their show. "They deserve an explanation," she said.

I objected. "They're just a bunch of jerks, Mom."

"No," she said. "They're good people who've just been hurt."

Every time I tried to make a derogatory comment about them, my mom defended them.

We finally arrived. My soft-spoken, little mother tried to explain. The response was a cold blast of angry words and disappointment. They wouldn't listen; they were angry and upset and had no desire to change their feelings. They accused the judges of playing favorites. My mother answered with sympathy and understanding. She was kind and complimentary to them and their efforts. She thanked the ward leaders for participating and putting on an excellent show. She refused to fight back at their railing. But at the same time she stood by the decision of the judges.

Finally we started home. "See, Mom," I said. "I told you they were poor losers. They're real jerks."

She wouldn't hear of it. Even though they had abused her to her face, she again defended them and expressed empathy for their feelings.

On this and many other occasions she showed love and patience to others regardless of how they treated her. When she knew what was needed, she acted on it. It was not something she had to consciously think about or work at. It was her true self. What an example she was to me.

Be ye kind one to another, tenderhearted.

EPHESIANS 4:32

ADAM'S GAME
MICHAEL J. GRAY

One day, my whole perception of Church sports changed. It had seemed that competition drove each team. Everyone wants to win, and no one wants to lose. But on this particular day, every boy was going to play. That's what the Young Men president told me. He said that my son Adam could play.

Adam is twelve and a very important part of our family and of his deacons quorum in the Brentwood Ward in the Portland Oregon Stake. Adam has been diagnosed as being borderline autistic. He also has a seizure disorder. With these conditions, he is developmentally delayed and is working on improving his motor skills.

Today, though, Adam knew he was going to play basketball on the deacons team. He was excited, and he kept asking about it all the way to the stake center. "Adam's basketball game?" would be his question. My reply was, "Yes, your game."

I had some concerns. How would the deacons respond with Adam on the court? Would they be careful with him out there? Would they let him handle the ball?

Everything began as church games should, with an opening prayer. Each team was receiving last-minute instructions from their coaches that when Adam was on the court there would be special concern for his safety. No overly aggressive moves would be tolerated.

The game began. With about two minutes to go in the first quarter, the coach called for Adam. With some coaxing Adam went to the scorer's table and checked in. The official whistled him into the game.

At first, Adam played defense. Not knowing exactly what he should do, when everyone else ran to the other end of the floor, he did too, laughing all the way. Adam loves to run, especially when others are running with him.

At the two-minute mark of the second period, Adam again entered the game. With one minute left, our team had the ball out-of-bounds. Tyler received the ball from the referee to throw in. Adam, just a few feet away, was the only one open.

Tyler gently threw him the ball. Adam caught it, turned around, tucked the ball under his arm and ran. No one called traveling. He made his way through the players to the basket, took aim, and shot. The ball hit the rim and bounced off to one side. One of the opposing players picked it up and without hesitation handed the ball back to Adam.

Again Adam aimed and shot. Those watching used all the body language they could muster to help the ball go in. Another miss. The ball was given back to Adam. This time a basket. Everyone cheered the biggest cheer of the game. Adam exchanged high fives with his team and the opposing team and the half ended.

In the third quarter, with two minutes to play, Adam was in again. The ball was back in his hands, and Adam did what he knew how to do. He ran toward the basket, took aim, and shot, with young men standing and cheering him on. They rooted for him until he made the basket. Another round of cheers and high fives.

The score and point spread had no meaning that day. Everyone won. Those who watched, especially a grateful father, and those who played will always have this special game to remember forever.

Michael J. Gray, "Adam's Game," © by Intellectual Reserve, Inc. Previously published in the *New Era*, Nov. 1997, 44–45.

Every one that hath forsaken houses, or brethren, or sisters, or father, or mother, or wife, or children, or lands, for my name's sake, shall receive an hundredfold, and shall inherit everlasting life.

MATTHEW 19:29

DEAD TO HIS FAMILY
MICHAEL R. MORRIS

Vadakke Madom Harihara Subramoniam Iyer had hoped his father and mother would attend his wedding last year or at least approve of his decision to marry. He misses their love and counsel.

But as a convert to the Church, "Ganesh" is dead to his parents. In their eyes, their firstborn son disgraced them. They acknowledge Ganesh only during an annual "death anniversary" ceremony. They have cut him out of the family inheritance and have ended all association and communication.

Such is the price of Church membership for many Hindu converts—especially if, like Ganesh, they descend from orthodox Hinduism's priestly Brahman lineage.

Ganesh first met the missionaries—Laurel and Nathel Hill of Ogden, Utah—in 1986 in the town of Goa, overlooking the Arabian Sea on India's west coast. Ironically, Ganesh's initial interest in the Church stemmed from his involvement with friends working formally to establish India as a religious state. The group sent Ganesh to gather information about the Church and to discourage the Hills—who were holding discussions in their home because open proselyting was then illegal in India.

"I loved Christians, but I hated them for the work they were doing," Ganesh says. "We felt that they were polluting India, and we wanted to stop conversions to Christianity."

In discussions with the missionaries, Ganesh says, "We talked about everything in the world except what I had come for. Literally, each time we spoke I forgot what I went to talk to them about. After three visits, I gave up." During one visit, the Hills gave Ganesh a copy of the Book of Mormon and taught him to pray. Shortly thereafter, while on a three-month work assignment outside Goa, Ganesh became ill and turned to prayer in seeking to recover his health.

Upon returning to Goa, Ganesh began taking the missionary discussions after work, keeping the Hills up late at night with questions. After the fifth discussion, he accepted an invitation from Elder Hill to be baptized. "Elder Hill hugged me, and we both wept," Ganesh says.

When friends found out about his baptism, they were at first incredulous, then angry. "I told them I was not happy with the work I was doing earlier, but that I was happy now," Ganesh says. "And then I got the same treatment that I caused others to get, which means I got beaten up on the road, twice, very nicely."

Ganesh was fired from his job and lost his apartment. His parents were equally unforgiving, especially when Ganesh told them that he planned to serve a mission.

"They said, 'You no longer have any rights in the family; you don't belong to us. We don't want you to be a member of our family. You became a Christian missionary. We can never forgive you for that.' "

Last year when Ganesh's mother became seriously ill and was expected to die, the family posted guards outside her hospital room to keep Ganesh from seeing her. Ganesh, however, was able to walk unrecognized into his mother's room. While there he asked her if she would like a blessing.

" 'You, bless me?' she asked, because in Hinduism, only the elder ones bless the younger ones," says Ganesh. After he explained the purpose of priesthood blessings, his mother asked him for a blessing. Ganesh felt prompted to bless her with renewed health, and within days she was released from the hospital.

"She appreciates what I have done. She told me, 'I know that you are in the right place for you.' That's enough for me."

Ganesh's father, however, feels that if God had wanted Ganesh to be a member of the Church, his son would have been born into the Church.

"He had a lot of hopes tied up in me," Ganesh says. "He thought I would take care of and bring up the family's name, I being the first son. As per his calculation, I am not doing that. But I told him I believe that God has a purpose for me: to put me where I was and to put me where I am now. I know, because of my patriarchal blessing, that my ancestors will be grateful for the work I will do for them."

Prayer and the support from fellow Church members have

helped Ganesh through his trials. The blessings of the gospel, the conversion of his wife, Elizabeth, before their marriage, and the knowledge that God lives, he says, have compensated for what he has lost.

Today, Ganesh serves as a leader in the Bangalore Second Branch and as executive secretary in the Bangalore district presidency. He speaks several languages and is helping translate Church materials into his native tongue, Tamil.

"I will be forever grateful to my Heavenly Father because, to use my earthly father's words, 'I am what I am and not what I was,'" Ganesh says. "I believe that I have a calling, that I have something special to do. All these troubles, all these problems, all this agony I have gone through are given to me so that I can stay strong."

Jesus said, "No man, having put his hand to the plough, and looking back, is fit for the kingdom of God" (Luke 9:62). For Ganesh, the field ahead may still be strewn with stones, but he is holding fast to the plow.

And he is not looking back.

Slightly modified from Michael R. Morris, "India: A Season of Sowing," © by Intellectual Reserve, Inc. Previously published in the *Ensign*, July 1995, 46–47.

"YOU DON'T OWE
THIS MONEY ANYMORE"
DARLA BUTTERS

Life was good for us in the mid-seventies. My husband,
Derek, was getting established in his construction company and
had just taken on a partner, named Tom, to help share the load.
Business was booming. Derek was getting to be well known for his
quality work and fair prices. After having had a rough start financially, we felt like life was finally starting to go our way.

Then, on my birthday, two people from the Internal Revenue
Service stood at my doorstep and informed me they had a war-
rant for the arrest of both myself and my husband. We were
shocked. The tax money had supposedly been paid, but on inves-
tigation we discovered that we had not been as careful or attentive to our bookkeeping as we should have been. So began a long
battle with the IRS, trying to play catch-up with past taxes and
at the same time trying to deal with many thousands of dollars in
late penalty fees.

In the meantime, Derek and Tom were working with a developer who was putting in ten homes in the north end of the valley. When our first draw for money went in, the developer of the project told us he was having some trouble with the bank. He promised to get the money to us soon and asked us to keep working. When the next draw was missed, Derek and Tom began to get extremely nervous. The developer still promised to pay them, but by that point he owed them well over two hundred thousand dollars.

Within weeks Derek and Tom received a notice that the developer had filed bankruptcy, leaving Derek and Tom owing all that money to suppliers and subcontractors. Derek and Tom worked diligently for more than a year to try to pay off their huge debt. They tried to work with their creditors, but the economy had slowed way down, and it was difficult to make the payments. At the same time, interest rates soared to over eighteen percent. As a result, we both lost our homes to the bank. Derek and I prayed fervently together to know how to face this overwhelming financial fiasco. Bankruptcy seemed to be our only option, but the decision weighed heavily on Derek, leaving him depressed and withdrawn.

Derek had a few jobs still running to keep food on the table. Then Tom fell from a thirty-foot roof, seriously injuring his back and putting him in the hospital for many weeks. Derek gave half of his paycheck to Tom to help his family get along. When Tom came home, Derek still visited him and helped him out financially, even when it meant our family would not have enough.

Finally, Tom and Derek agreed to end their partnership. Soon thereafter, Tom moved out of state—but not before he did a number of unethical things, to the detriment of their company. And in the process, Tom let many people down who were expecting him to follow through on prior commitments and money newly owed.

After the bankruptcy, Derek went down the list of all his creditors. He methodically contacted each one, asking if he could do something to repay them. The banker was the most surprised of all when he understood what Derek proposed to do. "You've taken out bankruptcy," he said. "You don't owe this money anymore. It's unheard of for you to try to repay it."

But Derek was undeterred. For the next several years, he made time after working twelve to fifteen hours a day, six days a week, to go and work off his debts.

The banker became a fast friend. He admired Derek's honesty, integrity, and tenacity and said he would give him credit and work with him anytime.

As for the IRS problem, Derek called to make arrangements to pay off that debt as well, along with the huge penalties that had accrued. The old caseworker had passed away, and the new man informed Derek that all past history had been deleted from their files. "Our records show that you owe us exactly nothing," he said.

"That's not right," Derek responded. "I know I owe tens of thousands of dollars to you, plus penalties."

"Not anymore," the caseworker said. "We have no record of this debt. Your case is officially closed."

I know Heavenly Father loves us and knows our hearts. Derek is such a hero in my eyes and in the eyes of many others. Over the years he has always showed complete honesty in all his dealings with his fellowman, and he has been blessed immensely for his integrity.

I am thankful for my hero, my husband, and my friend. He has never held a grudge against any man, friend or foe, and I know he would help out any of them in any need—yes, even Tom. I will be eternally grateful for his love, concern, and constant example of pure goodness through the past thirty years of our lives together.

They were all young men, . . . who were true at all times.

ALMA 53:20

BEFORE THE MOMENT OF CRISIS
ED AND PATRICIA PINEGAR

A young boy . . . early in his life had made a promise to God that he would never do anything to hurt his mother. Later, after he had grown older, he . . . made another promise that he would never do anything to offend God. Armed with that dual determination he was eventually confronted with a significant temptation.

His high school football team had won a game, and the players and some other fellows had gathered at a house where they were basking in the joy of victory. When one of the boys asked if he could have a drink of water, the host of the party invited him to help himself. Opening the kitchen cupboard to get a glass, he noticed a bottle of cooking wine on a shelf.

"Hey, you guys. Look what I've found! It's almost full! Let's see what wine really tastes like."

With their curiosity aroused and being in a jubilant mood, many of the boys exclaimed, "Yeah, let's do it!"

Only one boy expressed any reservation. "Hey, guys, we shouldn't do this. It isn't right, and besides, the wine isn't ours. You know darn well we shouldn't do this."

Then the abuse began. "What are you, a goody-goody? Hey, flake off, man. We don't need you telling us what to do."

The young man now had to make a decision. "If I drink it, I'll be their pal. If I don't, they'll make fun of me."

Just then he noticed a boy standing in the doorway. The boy was younger, a deacon in the ward where he was a priest. Recalling the promises he had already made—to his God and to his mother—the older boy put his arm around the younger boy's shoulders and said, "Come on, we don't belong here." They walked away with taunts ringing in their ears but feeling satisfied that they had chosen to do what was right.

You have to wonder what the outcome might have been had the priest not internalized his values and made a decision prior to the temptation—before the moment of crisis.

From "Avoiding Temptation," in Wright, *Why Say No When the World Says Yes?* 10–11.

By love serve one another.

WHICH ONE THE HERO?
JACOB S. SCHAFFER

When Jordan was adopted by a family in our stake, at first he seemed normal in his development. But at about nine years of age he began to fall behind physically. After considerable study and diagnosis, doctors finally determined that Jordan had a new variety of creeping dystrophy in which the nerves slowly atrophy until no messages reach the muscles. It was such a new discovery that they named the syndrome after him, Jordan's Syndrome.

By the time he was in high school, Jordan was quite small compared to the rest of the students. He weighed about ninety pounds. He could still talk fairly well and had a fun personality. But his walk was halting and unsure, and his hands were curled inward, limiting their usefulness.

Because of his disabilities, Jordan didn't have much of a social life. Yet he wanted so much to be like the other kids, going on dates and doing fun things with friends.

It was during these high school years that another boy in our stake, Spencer, began to take a personal interest in helping

Jordan. And even though many others also helped, the service given by Spencer was amazing.

When Spencer went on a date he would take Jordan; at times he even lined up the girl who would be Jordan's date. They went to movies and parties together. They went swimming together. As they got older they went to a single adult ward together. Jordan loved it.

As time passed Jordan's disease took its toll, and he grew more and more dependent on others. When they double dated to a dance, Spencer would hold Jordan up so he could dance. Sometimes Jordan would even ride on Spencer's strong shoulders as they danced. After Jordan was confined to a wheelchair, Spencer would push Jordan around so he could still participate.

When Spencer turned nineteen he accepted a call to serve a mission. Others stepped in to help while Spencer was gone, and somehow Jordan made it. But Jordan missed his special friend.

Finally Spencer's two-year mission was over. Jordan rode to the airport with Spencer's family. They helped him into the airport and onto the concourse to wait for his buddy. When Spencer approached, in Jordan's enthusiasm he tried to stand up to hug his friend. Instead, he ended up crumpled on the floor. Spencer raced to Jordan, picked him up in his arms, and carried him down the concourse.

Spencer was shocked to see Jordan's deteriorated condition. He realized that Jordan would not last long in this life. It was then that Spencer made a promise to his Heavenly Father: he would do all he could to take care of Jordan for the rest of Jordan's mortal life.

One of Jordan's dreams was to go to Disneyland. It seemed impossible. But Spencer assured Jordan's parents that he would take good care of Jordan at Disneyland—that all would be well with him. With the help of another young man, Jordan and Spencer set out in a car for the long trip. It was a sacrifice not only of time and money for the two escorts; they also had to help Jordan with all of his needs. They helped him move from place to place. They even gave him his baths. But despite the difficulty, it was a wonderful experience for the three of them—and Jordan was thrilled.

About five years later Jordan's body died. It was a bittersweet experience for Spencer to lose his friend. On the one hand, he knew that Jordan would now be free from his debilitating physical limitations. On the other hand, he had made a promise to bless Jordan—and he had kept that promise. But Spencer knew that he himself had been blessed as much as Jordan had—and maybe more. Some would say Spencer was a true hero to Jordan. Spencer would say that Jordan was the hero. Both are right.

*Verily my sabbaths ye shall keep: for it is a sign
between me and you . . . ; that ye may know that
I am the Lord that doth sanctify you.*

EXODUS 31:13

HE WORKED FOR HIS FRIENDS
TODD W. LAMBERT

After his mission, Peter Gallagher began looking for a job. He wanted to work some place where he would have a chance to use the Spanish he had learned on his mission. Soon he found such a job working at a nice restaurant in a large hotel where tourists and people from many parts of the world stopped to eat.

During Peter's interview with the manager, she informed him that the restaurant was open on Sundays. "Is that going to be a problem for you?" He told her that he wouldn't work on Sundays. She answered, "Well, maybe we can work something out."

After Peter started work he kept waiting for the manager to "work something out," but she never did. Then she began to schedule Peter to work on Sundays. Every Saturday he informed her that he would not be able to work on Sunday. This continued for quite some time.

Peter showed up to work on time every day he was scheduled, except Sundays. He was reliable in his work, enjoyed his job, and even got to speak Spanish to some of the clientele. It was hard work, but he got along well with his fellow employees and had fun.

But the manager began to get upset at Peter for not working on Sundays. Sometimes she would tell him what a great employee he was and would compliment him for his dependability and for how well he was getting along with the other employees and the customers. Other times she would get angry and swear at him for his refusal to come in on Sundays.

Then Jamil, the headwaiter, was in a car accident and was unable to work. The manager asked Peter to cover for Jamil for several days, including Sunday.

Peter considered the matter and decided that he would do the work. But on Sunday he would not clock in or out, so he would not be working for money on the Sabbath. Then at the end of that Sunday's work, Peter did an amazing thing. He took all the tips he had earned that day and divided them equally among the other waiters. The waiters were confused. "Why would you give us your money? You earned it," they said.

"I wasn't working for money today," he answered. "I was working to help my friends in a time of need."

Eventually the manager called Peter into her office. "I know you have a commitment to your church," she said. "But I have a business to run. Either you will work on Sundays, like everybody else, or you're not going to work for me anymore."

"You don't understand," he said. "I not only have a commitment to my church, but more importantly, I have a commitment to my God. And he has commanded me to keep the Sabbath day holy."

Peter turned in his name tag, his apron, and his time card and then left.

To this day, Peter has worked only one Sunday in his life, and that was for his friends.

Giving all diligence, add to your . . . brotherly kindness charity.

2 PETER 1:5, 7

MY MEMORY TREES
FELECIA ANGUS AS TOLD TO BARBARA JEAN JONES

It was supposed to be a great day. It started out with Mom making a wonderful breakfast for Alan and me in honor of my eleventh birthday.

Alan was my twelve-year-old brother, but he was also my best friend. We got along so well that other people couldn't believe we were brother and sister. We hardly ever fought, and we shared a lot of our thoughts, too.

Halfway through the school day I received a message from my parents to go to a friend's house after school. All afternoon I let my imagination have a good time thinking about the surprise party my parents must be planning.

But that changed as soon as I got to my friend's house and was told that Alan was sick and in the hospital. Alan had always been very healthy, so I was really surprised and worried.

Later, my parents picked me up at my friend's house, and we rode home in silence. I was even more confused when we got home and there were neighbors and ward members everywhere doing our chores and making my birthday dinner.

My parents took me into my room and told me that Alan had died suddenly of a heart attack while at school. We hadn't known it, but Alan had a birth defect in his heart. Devastated, I screamed uncontrollably. It would be a long time before I could accept the fact that my brother was gone.

Over the next few days we received several cards and plants in remembrance of Alan. But the thing I remember most was that some of Alan's friends brought over and planted two fruit trees— a plum for Alan and an apple for me. The fact that those boys remembered my birthday along with remembering Alan made me feel very special.

The days, weeks, and months passed in a numbing blur. I had always looked forward to birthdays, but as my twelfth one drew near, it was hard to be excited for it. How could I be happy on the day I had lost my best friend and brother?

On the first anniversary of Alan's death, was I ever surprised when three of the boys who had planted the trees showed up on my doorstep with a bouquet of flowers for my birthday. They came in and visited with my family, really lifting our spirits. I didn't have Alan to share his life with me, but I did have his three friends. They became my heroes.

Year after year, those three boys continued to come on my birthday, sometimes bringing flowers or sometimes brownies, always visiting with our family. I never expected them to come all those years. I cannot even begin to think of words to express how much it has meant to me.

When the boys' senior year came, we attended their high

school and seminary graduations. The ceremonies were nice, but all the talk of graduation, college, and missions was a little hard for me—probably because those were the things Alan would have been doing if he had been here.

Shortly after we got home, the doorbell rang. We opened the door to find a big group of students from what would have been Alan's graduating seminary class. There among the smiling faces were my three heroes. One of them made a small speech, and they gave us an honorary seminary graduation certificate with Alan's name on it.

My tree and Alan's tree continue to grow up together and now sprout beautiful blossoms. Although the trees weren't much bigger than I was when the boys planted them, today they stretch way above my head. Whenever I look at them, I think of Alan, of three boys now grown to young men, and of the message those boys brought to me from Heavenly Father that I am never alone or forgotten.

The three boys won't be coming on my birthday for the next couple of years. But by the time they return from their missions, I hope I'll be able to share with them the first fruits of the trees they planted for me.

Slightly modified from Felecia Angus as told to Barbara Jean Jones, "My Memory Trees," © by Intellectual Reserve, Inc. Previously published in the *New Era*, July 1999, 12–14.

Charity envieth not; charity vaunteth not itself.

1 CORINTHIANS 13:4

THE RED SHOES
MAURINE CARLILE

I was raised in a small town that had a great love for the performing arts, though opportunities to perform came rarely. But I was lucky enough to be associated with a few truly great individuals who taught me some essential life's lessons. One such lesson that vividly stands out in my mind, I learned when I was in high school.

One of my best friends, Susan, was extremely talented. She had been able to use her talents in many ways—mostly performing outside of our small community. She was what is called in the theater a "triple threat," meaning that she was talented not only as an actress but also as a singer and dancer. This made her especially adept in musical theater. She had filled major roles in many musicals, but none in our community. Performing was one of her greatest loves.

When we were seniors in high school, our drama teacher announced she was going to present the musical *The Wizard of Oz*. We were all excited and talked about which part we dared try out for. Susan really wanted to audition for the part of Dorothy. It was a part she had always wanted to play.

A few days before the auditions were held, the drama teacher approached Susan privately and said, "Susan, you have had many opportunities to use your talents. I think it would be best if you didn't try out for this play so others will have a chance to perform. Instead, I'd like you to choreograph the munchkin scene."

Susan was devastated. But, as the days passed, I watched in wonder as Susan helped another of our friends, Julie, prepare to audition for the part of Dorothy. Susan spent many hours coaching her and practicing with her. Both Julie and Susan were thrilled when Julie got the part.

The next six weeks were devoted to preparing for the show—rehearsing, sewing costumes, learning dance routines, and building scenery. Susan created a wonderful dance for the munchkin scene and tried to help in any other way she could.

When the costuming was almost finished, we held a dress rehearsal, so the cast could get used to moving while costumed. I especially watched for the munchkin scene—and quickly saw that it wasn't going to work. The costumes encumbered the dancers so severely they could hardly move. There wasn't time to start over on either costumes or choreography, so the director cut most of Susan's choreography. Susan felt terrible but didn't complain.

Finally, just two days before the show opened, everyone was feeling stressed. One of the missing finishing touches was

Dorothy's famous pair of red shoes. Julie had been asked to provide her own shoes but had been unable to do so.

The next day at school I heard an amazing story. At about 10:30 the night before, Susan had called Julie and asked permission to stop by Julie's house. Julie hesitated—she was pretty busy, she said—but she guessed it would be all right if Susan stayed for just a minute.

Susan showed up at Julie's door with a box in her hands. In the box was a beautiful pair of shoes, dyed red, with sparkling glitter all over them. I could hardly believe it. How had Susan found the time? Where had she gotten the shoes? How could she do this when she herself had wanted that part so much?

That night, as I was trying to get to sleep, I started to think about how Susan had handled this challenge: coaching Julie for the auditions, seeing her get the part, having the director drastically cut the only scene she'd been able to work on, and finally recognizing the need for the shoes and providing them. I wondered what I would have done if I'd been in Susan's place.

The last chapter of this story took place after one of the performances. A number of theatrical people from outside our community came to see the show—people who knew about Susan's abilities and experience. I overheard one of these people say: "Susan, you were simply treated unfairly in all of this. Aren't you angry about it?"

I listened quietly, waiting for Susan to agree with him.

Instead, she just smiled. "Isn't it wonderful that Julie had this opportunity?" she said—and I could tell she meant it.

It was an example and a spirit of unselfishness I will never forget.

He that loveth his brother abideth in the light.

1 JOHN 2:10

THE QUIET REACHING OUT
NAOMI RICHARDS

I know being a teenager is hard for almost everyone, but I had an additional challenge during those years. My father was a career officer in the U.S. Army, and due to his reassignments, our family relocated every two or three years. Because of our frequent moves and my natural tendency toward shyness, I made few close friends as I was growing up. One of the few friends I did have, and also one of the few constants in my life, was my cousin Lindsay.

My high school years were spent in Stuttgart, Germany. They were the hardest years of my life. Soon after I graduated from high school, my father retired, and we left Germany to live in Salt Lake City. Another move, but at least we would now be stationary—and I would be living near my cousins.

I had been accepted to attend the University of Utah, but I had always attended small military schools, and the thought of attending a large school with so many students on such an enormous campus was totally intimidating to me. In addition, our whole family was trying to make the difficult adjustment from military to civilian life, resulting in many family conflicts. I was feeling discouraged and unsettled. I had little confidence and felt lost. To make things worse, I was also struggling with my testimony.

Lindsay was a sophomore at the University of Utah. She was also very involved with the LDS Institute of Religion on campus and was a member of the Salt Lake Institute choir council. She had been called to serve as the choir's publicity director. Lindsay was very artistic and talented, but for some reason she felt she needed help in her calling. She asked me to act as her unofficial assistant.

I resisted the idea because I felt stressed and insecure. But Lindsay insisted that she needed a helper—and said it had to be me. Finally I agreed.

But the more I thought about going to school—coupled with family problems, my flagging testimony, and my overall feeling of discouragement—I finally decided to drop the whole idea of school and spend a year trying to get my feet under me. I called Lindsay to tell her about my plans.

Her response surprised me. "I can't do this without you," she said. "Even if you don't go to school, I need you."

I continued to feel reluctant. I didn't understand why she needed help. She was so "in charge," so capable. Besides, I knew there were other people she could ask. Why did it have to be me? I told her some of my feelings.

But Lindsay just wouldn't take "no" for an answer. "There's no one else who can help me the way you can," she said.

Again, I finally agreed. How could I say no to my cousin and best friend? I said I would do it.

Her insistence—and my acquiescence—simply changed my

life. Lindsay and I grew closer than ever. We double dated, attended classes, went to rehearsals, performed in our concerts, did publicity work, and even participated in a performing tour together. With her encouragement I auditioned for the Salt Lake Institute Show Choir and the Mormon Youth Symphony Chorus and was accepted into both.

My testimony returned and blossomed. I began to realize I had many God-given talents and had much to offer. I came out of my shell, surviving and even thriving in the very year I had thought would be the worst of my life.

In addition to finding myself, I found something else. One day I noticed a certain handsome tenor singing in the choir. Why hadn't I been aware of him before?

Soon, he noticed that I was noticing. We dated, became engaged, were married in the temple, and now have three sons. My husband and I both hold callings in our ward. I have a strong testimony and a deep love for my Heavenly Father and my Savior Jesus Christ. I have taken my vocal talent in new directions through private vocal study.

As topping on the cake, some time after our marriage, my husband's younger brother dated and married my younger sister!

It was a small thing Lindsay did. She had seen the desperation in my life, thought and prayed about it, kept herself open to the Spirit, and found a way to help me that I could not refuse. She could not have known how far-reaching her simple act would be, blessing my life and my family's forever. But she did the little thing she could do, bringing big results and becoming one of my heroes forever.

BLESSED IN OUR BURDENS
SUZANNE LEE

For most of our married life, my husband, Alan, has had medical problems that have made it difficult for him to work full time. He has tried a number of different jobs—some part time and some temporary—but because of his health he hasn't been able to keep any of them for long. This has particularly been true for the last dozen or more years. I have worked myself, but to say that our income has been inadequate would be an understatement. As a result we were always poor. Every Christmas was a nightmare of wondering what we would do.

And yet in our trials, we have been surrounded by rescuing heroes, ready and anxious to help us, always there just when we needed them. For example, one year a woman hired me to help clean her invalid mother's house. She paid me well for it, and I found a special new friend in her mother—an extra bonus. When the mother died, she willed her car to me. I was astounded. What a wonderful, unexpected blessing! It was a very nice little two-year-old Subaru with only 35,000 miles on it. That was almost ten years ago. I am still using that car. What keeps it running? A backyard neighbor who is a Subaru mechanic. He takes care of all the maintenance on my car and only charges for parts, plus a little for his labor.

Another example: One birthday, I woke up feeling angry, bitter, and depressed. I resented that I wasn't able to have "things" like most everyone else did. Even though it wasn't logical, I felt that I must not be worthy.

As my birthday progressed and others were nice to me, I wondered why. Didn't they know that I was not worthy of being loved? But by the end of the day I was overwhelmed by the tokens of love I had received—cards, flowers, a cake, and presents. Friends and family called to wish me a happy birthday. My children did sweet things to cheer and bless me. In the afternoon I received a birthday letter from my parents. Inside was a check for the very amount we needed to replace our recently broken television set. The money had been given to my mom for Christmas, but she wanted me to have it. I sat and cried as I read their letter and felt their sacrifice. It was the last straw in the love I was receiving. It helped in the healing process. I knew that I was loved, that I *was* worthy of love—and that my Father in Heaven loved me too.

Many other miracles have come from my family. Over the years different brothers have contributed in different ways. Some have given us large sums of money. One year a brother gave us money for coats. He paid for new glasses for one of our sons. He sent cash. He provided work. He gave us an old truck. Another brother gave us a large sum of money that they had been saving to buy new carpet for their house. He loaned us a car. He paid for us to come visit him in another state for a vacation. A third brother invited me to help him with a project he was doing at his work. We were anxious to have the extra income, and the job lasted for several years. My parents have loaned us much money over the years, and my dad has always found imaginative, practical ways for me to pay it back.

The Church has sent heroes as well. Sometimes the bishop has helped us with bills, helped with house payments so we wouldn't lose our home, and provided us with food from the bishops' storehouse. Visiting teachers and home teachers and neighbors have provided help at crucial times. Alan's priesthood quorum has fasted for him and put their arms around him in love.

One week our Sunday School teacher invited the class to share stories of the blessing of tithing. I raised my hand. "Our whole life is a testimony of the blessing of tithing," I said. "By all rights we should be living on the streets, not in a comfortable home with furniture and a car and clothing and food. But the Lord has sent his blessings to us again and again."

As I look back over the years, I must indeed acknowledge the hand of the Lord in our lives. His miracles have come virtually every day: an unexpected box of groceries on the doorstep, an encouraging telephone call, repairs at a fraction of what they should have cost, a sweet and comforting reassurance from the Spirit, a reminder of the love of God for *me*. Sometimes just getting through the week is difficult. Sometimes I wonder how much more I can bear. But then someone else sacrifices for me and my family, and I know that the Lord is mindful of us, that he is watching over us, and that he will always bless us according to his wisdom—even if the blessing he sends is not what I asked for.

"HE SHOWED US WHAT COURAGE IS"
JANA ERICKSON

Jeffrey Hannay was born to be a fireman. A third-generation firefighter, he was part of an elite brotherhood of men and women in the Salt Lake County Fire Department who are united by a bond of trust, dedication, and service—a group deeply committed to taking care of their own.

Nearly everyone in the department knew the Hannay family. Jeffrey's brother was a firefighter, his father was a battalion chief, and his grandfather was a volunteer fireman. At the age of thirty-one, Jeff had it all. He had completed a full-time mission for The Church of Jesus Christ of Latter-day Saints. He had married his beautiful wife, Stacy, in the Salt Lake Temple and had three young children he adored. He had great friends and a strong extended family that spent many happy hours together. He had a natural ability for sports and loved fishing, water skiing, baseball, and basketball. He had a college degree and a new home. He had completed training as a paramedic and had a career he enjoyed, saving lives for a living. He also had a grapefruit-size cancerous tumor in his abdomen.

For five years following his diagnosis, Jeff and his family lived a roller-coaster existence of brutal chemotherapy, surgery, radiation, and joyous remission—always followed by a dreaded recurrence, more chemotherapy, more surgery, and more radiation. His fellow firefighters supported him from the beginning. A few weeks into the first round of chemotherapy, Jeff lost his hair. His coworkers decided to show their support by shaving their heads. More than seventy firefighters—including some whom Jeff had never met—lined up to shed their locks and donate $25 apiece to help Jeff pay for medical expenses. One firefighter explained, "My wife called and tried to talk me out of it. My kids called to talk me out of it. But when he walked in, and we were all standing there with our heads shaved and the tears started coming down his face, that was it—it was worth it."

During the years that followed, county firefighters and paramedics worked Jeff's shifts while he was in the hospital or receiving treatments. They mowed his lawn, chopped firewood, and shoveled snow. They came to sporting events to watch Jeff's children play. They gave financial and moral support during the tough times, visiting him at home and in the hospital. They offered vacation days to supplement Jeff's sick leave, and their wives volunteered to tend his children so Stacy could be by his side when he was in the hospital.

Jeff's battle was long and difficult, but his courage and determination were greater. He continued to work as a paramedic, always on time for his shifts, and always setting an example for others of personal commitment and dedication. Throughout the department there was a renewed sense of duty—other fire-fighters said, "If Jeff can be to work sick as he is, I can be there with my little problems." Even while cancer ravaged his body, Jeff set training records for physical strength and ability. He never missed an opportunity to assist someone else in need, often performing physically demanding jobs such as helping friends or neighbors move and putting in landscaping. He was simply grateful for the chance to return some of the service that he had received. At church, Jeff taught the priests quorum in his ward, providing an unequaled example of character and faith to the young men he served. In spite of his terminal illness, Jeff refused to give up. He was determined to make each day count. "His life and his struggle helped each one of us to keep our own difficulties in perspective," said County Fire Chief Don Berry. "He fought the good fight and taught us all something along the way."

When Jeff passed away just twelve days after working his last shift, more than three hundred firefighters with black shields covering their badges attended the memorial service to pay tribute to one of their own. Behind the scenes, a trust for Jeff's children was quietly established by his colleagues. His partner, Troy Prows, devotedly finished the home repairs that he and Jeff had begun a few weeks earlier. Yard work was done, letters and flowers were sent, and many, many visits were made to ensure that the needs of Jeff's wife and children were met.

Jeffrey Hannay left a legacy of service received and returned in the face of incredible odds. "He accomplished in thirty-six years what many people fail to do in eighty or more," wrote Elder

Glen L. Rudd, a family friend. Added County Fire Chief Don Berry, "Even after he was gone he taught me why I became a fire-fighter. . . . He showed us what courage is."

But to Jeff's family, the true heroes are the dedicated fire-fighters who stood by him for five long years, never failing to come through at the right time and place. In the words of Jeff's wife, Stacy, "I will always have a deep love and appreciation for the fire department. I will always have tears of pride and happiness when I see a fire truck, engine, or rescue vehicle going by."

Note: March 5, 2002, marked the one-year anniversary of Jeff's passing. On that day, a beautiful arrangement of lovely spring flowers was delivered to the Hannay home. Stacy was not surprised to learn they had been sent by firefighters.

Be strong and of a good courage; be not afraid,
neither be thou dismayed: for the Lord thy God is with thee.

JOSHUA 1:9

A DIFFERENT KIND OF COURAGE
WAYNE B. LYNN

It happened in a rather common place, for that seems to be where most heroic deeds happen. It happened in a stake priesthood meeting on a hot July afternoon. The chapel was filled to overflowing, and the partition doors leading into the cultural hall had been opened to accommodate the large body of the priesthood. A special spirit seemed to be with us that day as our beloved stake president presided over us and conducted the affairs of the stake.

One lad who appeared to be about the age of a priest sat in a rather conspicuous place on the stand near the stake presidency. I had correctly guessed that he was to take part on the program, and I sympathized with his contained nervousness.

Soon the president announced the young man as the next speaker. He arose quietly and walked the short distance to the stand. His outward composure was calm, but my vantage point near the front of the room permitted me a view of the quivering hands that told of the fear to be conquered.

Taking a deep breath, he began to speak. It was quickly obvious that he had spent much time in preparation. An occasional glance at his notes was all that was required. I began to relax a little in my apprehension for him, but then I noticed that his speech was beginning to come faster and faster. Words were coming so fast that they were being repeated unnecessarily. In the middle of his next sentence he began to stammer. This increased his nervousness to the degree that his stammering increased, making him entirely speechless.

A sympathetic silence filled the room. I longed to reassure him or indicate in some way my sympathy and understanding, but, like the others, I waited. I waited for him to surrender and perhaps try again another day.

I could see the youth waging an inward battle as he stood there before us. Then it happened. He squared his shoulders and girded himself to the task, uttering, as nearly as I can recall, these words: "Brethren, I ask for an interest in your faith and prayers that I might have sureness of speech."

It was as if I had seen a miracle. He began again to speak, slowly, deliberately, but with sureness and conviction. His young voice rang out in a message that thrilled my soul. It is not his words I remember, but stamped indelibly upon my memory is the message of the boy himself.

Somehow, I will never feel the same again when I am called upon to perform a difficult task. Perhaps I can take a few steps up the same trail blazed by this brave young man, for he had climbed the mount of moral courage and stood unflinching upon its precipice.

His talk was soon completed. He gathered his notes and turned away from the stand, and for a moment I saw more than a young man in a white shirt. I saw a knight in shining armor with a sword at his side and a token of victory in his hand. The words of a song surged into my consciousness so strongly that they seemed to be crying out to be heard: "Behold! A royal army, with banner, sword, and shield, is marching forth to conquer on life's great battlefield. Its ranks are filled with soldiers, united, bold, and strong, who follow their Commander and sing their joyful song: Victory, victory!" (*Hymns*, no. 251.)

Lynn, *Lessons from Life*, 50–52.

By love serve one another.

GALATIANS 5:13

———

HARRY'S BLESSINGS
CAMILLE PARRY

Harry Kirkham came into the life of my grandma when they were both in the winter of their lives. Lucky for me, he and Grandma hit it off and decided to spend the rest of their lives together.

Three years later my mom called my grandmother, who by then lived in Las Vegas, to tell her she was going through a heartbreaking divorce. "We need a place to stay, Mom," she said. "Can we stay with you?"

Grandma was very reluctant. Their apartment was small— and, besides, it might not work for Harry, who had never had any children of his own. To make matters worse, Grandma and Mom often clashed and sparks flew.

Harry overheard the conversation and got on the phone. "Pat, you bring those kids and come live with us," he said. "It's okay."

Harry soon proved to be the father figure (or grandfather figure!) I so much needed in my life. He was willing to drive me to my many Church activities, even though he wasn't a member himself. He never tried to dissuade me from going to seminary or from doing the many other things that are part of being active in the Church. He was unselfish with his money. He wasn't the type to spoil us, but he always made sure we had juice and ice cream in the house. He and Grandma took us on many trips—to Yellowstone Park, to ghost towns, and to Arizona's Oak Creek Canyon, where we stayed in a quaint little cabin. All this even though he wasn't our "real" grandpa. But nothing could have made him more real in his blessings to me.

One of Harry's great gifts to us was his sense of humor. He could always make us laugh—a precious gift in a household that seemed to be filled with constant tension between my mother and grandmother. He loved to be silly for us. Once he put on Mom's fur hat, which made him look like a Russian cossack, draped some hippie beads over his neck, and posed for a picture with a poodle in his arm and a chimpanzee funny-lips look on his face. And I smile to think of the crazy dance he did around the living room, calling it his "bear dance." Harry's antics and light-hearted jokes and teasing distracted me from the harshness and disappointments of life. He was consistently good-natured and loving, with a knack for lightening the mood.

These are simple things, ordinary things, everyday things— but with them Harry changed my life. He helped give me stability in my life. He was a constant. He taught me not to take myself too seriously. He helped me to find the fun in a life that otherwise was hard and heavy. Harry was one of the only normal things about my childhood. And he did all this for a girl who was not even related to him, for a family who disrupted his lifestyle and, in some ways, surely must have gotten underfoot in his small home. He did this by taking a sacrifice he had willingly made and turning it into a blessing for all, himself included.

Years later, my husband and I named our precious third son after Harry. Since Harry has no living blood relatives, we wanted to honor him and thank him for his influence on me. Our son's name is Kirkham Atwell Parry—Kirkham after Harry Kirkham, and Atwell after the other wonderful father figure in our lives, my husband's father, Atwell Parry. Interestingly, Parry comes from the Welsh, where it means, literally, Son of Harry.

Every man should be honored in his station.

D&C 134:6

"YOU LISTEN TO OUR PROPHET"
Hugh W. Pinnock

Just last spring a group of high school students sat in a seminary class looking at their watches, hoping the class would soon end. They were not paying attention to what was going on. They were laughing and teasing and passing notes.

President Ezra Taft Benson's face appeared on the video they should have been watching. He was talking about the Book of Mormon. The noise continued. Suddenly, a young woman stood up, stepped to the front of the class, and, frightened, said as she pushed the pause button, "He is our prophet. He talks with Heavenly Father. He is telling us about the Book of Mormon, and we should listen."

Suddenly, every eye was focused on the front of the room as that lovely young lady turned the television set back on and quietly returned to her seat.

In talking with the seminary teacher a week or two later, he said, "In all the years that I have taught, I have never seen a class more reverent, more focused upon the things that matter, as the day when that young lady went to the front of the class and said, 'You listen to our prophet.' " She did it on her own. She did not wait for another.

From Pinnock, "Now Is the Time," *Ensign*, May 1989, 11.

He that hath mercy on the poor, happy is he.

PROVERBS 14:21

A GOOD BOY'S CRY FOR HELP
HOLLY GIVENS

Years ago, as our son was preparing to serve a mission, our family was in difficult financial straits. We had recently finished graduate school and had a family of six children to raise. My husband's three degrees had required great sacrifices, we had massive student loans to repay, and it seemed our car was always in the shop.

One night our son overheard us discussing our impossible finances. Later that evening I went into his room to say good night and found him crying. "I wish I could pay for my own mission!" he said. The words seemed to erupt from years of concern about our unending struggle. Mark was our saver, passing up treats and toys while other children indulged. He had received his Eagle Award at age thirteen; he was a self-motivator, responsible and kind. It broke my heart to see his troubled spirit. We'd always encouraged our children to save for the clothing they'd need on their missions, promising them that we would pay for the actual missions. But now he'd heard that we had no money.

I sorrowed for him, and in the depths of my soul I wished he weren't aware of the sacrifice his mission would mean for us. We had faith things would work out somehow—though we didn't know how, or at what cost—and we didn't want Mark to know of the possible trial that awaited us.

Then the Lord touched a heart for my son's sake, sending an angel to bless our lives. One day a letter with no return address arrived in the mail. It was addressed to our son, Mark Givens. Inside he found a cashier's check for $9,000, exactly what we would need for all of his monthly missionary payments. We were overcome with joy and relief and were astonished beyond measure. Who could be this generous? The blessing to me and my husband was obvious—and even though we had told Mark not to be concerned about the money for his mission, we could tell that he was relieved of a weighty burden. We had all experienced a true miracle of love and sacrifice; in turn, it strengthened our faith and desire to build other people's lives through service.

As the days passed, we looked around us at friends and family members, wondering who the anonymous donor might be. Could it be that person? we wondered, or that one? Our love for those around us increased. Our belief in the intrinsic good of man grew stronger. We saw many we felt could be capable of such a sacrifice of love.

Perhaps our hero will read this and know that his or her prompting to extend a hand was due to a good boy's cry for help to his Heavenly Father—and will learn of the reverberating blessings that continue in our home to this day.

Who then is willing to consecrate his
service this day unto the Lord?

HOW SHE SPENDS HER DAYS
H. BURKE PETERSON

Some of us may not understand what we really mean by service. This principle is illustrated by an experience that two of the early Apostles had after the Savior was resurrected. It is found in the book of Acts. Peter and John were going into the temple through the gate called Beautiful, and as they passed through the gate there sat a man who had been lame since he was born. He looked up and held out his hand, asking for alms; he was begging.

"And Peter, fastening his eyes upon him with John, said [speaking to the lame man], Look on us.

"And he gave heed unto them, expecting to receive something of them.

"Then Peter said, Silver and gold have I none; but such as I have give I thee: In the name of Jesus Christ of Nazareth rise up and walk.

"And he [meaning Peter] took him by the right hand, and lifted him up" (Acts 3:4–7).

With these words Peter gave us another secret. As you think

of service to others, remember the words, "Silver and gold have I none; but such as I have give I thee."

Some time ago I was attending a stake conference in the United States. The stake president met me at the airport, and we had an hour's drive to the stake center. As we were driving we talked about many things, and the conversation began to center on an individual who lived in the stake. The stake president told me about a young lady who had gone on a mission about twenty years before, and while there had contracted polio. She walked into the hospital in a city in New England to take some tests, and she never walked again. She was paralyzed. And he said, "For twenty years she's been paralyzed from her neck down; she's not able to move any muscles below her neck, except a few in her fingers. But she's an unusual young lady. She has a spirit that is something wonderful." Well, before stake conferences I always get a little nervous. Consequently I said, "I need to be built up, President; let's go by and see the young lady."

So we went by her home; she was living with her parents. We went into her room, and there she lay on a bed, surrounded by the equipment that would keep her interested and busy during the day. As I walked into the room, I saw a physically pitiful sight, but I felt a spirit that I have felt in very few places. I was overcome by her spirit. I began to ask her some questions. As she lay there I saw that she could move a few fingers on one hand and a few on the other, but she could not raise or lower her arms. She had an air pump on a table by her side. She would hold the tube in her hand and every few minutes would put it into her mouth.

It would blow air into her lungs. She would then turn away and her lungs would deflate. She did this several times an hour to keep the air moving into her body. And I said, "Tell me what you do during the day." I knew she had lain there for twenty years in this physical condition.

And her parents said, "We'll show you how she spends her days."

They brought a typewriter and put it in front of her on her bed. Her mother laid one of her daughter's hands on the typewriter keys, then she took the other and also laid it on the keys. The young lady then showed us how with these few fingers she would type. She said, "During the day I find those who are sick and discouraged and write poetry and letters to them and send them good wishes that will make them happy. I try to help those who are less fortunate than I am." There she lay with hardly anything physical going for her, but with a spirit that could perform miracles.

Next her parents brought a telephone and put it in her hands and moved it up to her ear and mouth. With two fingers, she punched the push-button dial. In this way she called those who were not as well off as she was and cheered them up during the day. Remember what Peter said: "Silver and gold have I none; but such as I have give I thee."

Peterson, A Glimpse of Glory, 93–96.

The integrity of the upright shall guide them.

PROVERBS 11:3

THE HUNTING TRIP
JOHN M. R. COVEY

My father loved hunting with his boys. He made it exciting, building our anticipation with the preparation of the equipment, planning the best locations, and the like. It took weeks of anticipation and effort to finally be ready for the hunt.

I will never forget one Saturday opening of the pheasant hunt. Dad, my older brother, and I were up at 4:00 A.M. We ate Mom's big, hearty breakfast, packed the car, and drove to our designated field by 6:00 A.M. We arrived early to stake out our spot before any others, anticipating the 8:00 A.M. opening hour.

As that hour drew near, other hunters were frantically driving around us, trying to find spots in which to hunt. As 7:40 arrived, we saw hunters driving into the fields. By 7:45 the firing had started—fifteen minutes before the official start. We looked at Dad. He made no move except to look at his watch, still waiting for 8:00 A.M. Soon the birds were flying. By 7:50 all hunters had moved into the fields and shots were everywhere.

Dad looked at his watch. He only said, "The hunt starts at eight o'clock A.M., boys." About three minutes before eight, four hunters drove into our spot and walked past us, into our field. We looked at Dad. He said: "The hunt starts for us at eight." At eight the birds were gone, but we started our drive into the field.

We didn't get any birds that day. We did get an unforgettable memory of a man, my ideal, who taught me absolute integrity and whom I fervently wanted to be like.

From Grassli, Packer, and Woodhead, *Dad, You're the Best!* 14.

Thy friends do stand by thee, and they shall
hail thee . . . with warm hearts and friendly hands.

D&C 121:9

"HOW I HATED THOSE GIRLS!"
NAME WITHHELD BY REQUEST

I came from a family of four. My mother was LDS, but my father was intolerant toward the Mormon Church. There was great discord, many arguments, and much bitterness in our home. My parents quarreled constantly, both verbally and physically.

We paid a price. At sixteen my older brother had been convicted on a narcotics charge and had been placed in a detention home. I was fourteen and headed down that same road.

I had been baptized at eight and had always attended Sunday School with my mother. Now, at fourteen, I went to church only to get out of the house and keep peace with my mom.

I'll never forget the first Sunday some girls from my Mutual class came around to invite me to Mutual. Four girls! Two of them were cheerleaders at Central Junior High where we all went to school. The other two girls I had, of course, seen at church and school and knew were popular and well liked.

How I hated those girls! I hated them because they were everything I wanted to be and couldn't. I was nothing, I was low-class—I knew it and I knew they knew it, too. I hated them all. I took their crummy little invitation note and smugly lied that I'd be sure to make it out to Mutual. Of course, I never went.

This story could have ended there. Those four girls had done their duty at the beginning of the year. I had been personally invited out to Mutual and had refused. What more could they do?

Fortunately for me, the story did not end there. In the months that followed, every Sunday one of those four girls would be at my door with an invitation. But she wouldn't just drop it off and leave. Each girl would stay and talk to me for at least an hour. At first we would talk about the weather and about Sunday School, which were the only two things I had in common with them, and then we would sit through eternal silences.

Gradually our conversations became closer. The girls always seemed so eager to listen to my ideas and problems. They never yelled at me or called me names. And yet I was still apprehensive and I still disliked them greatly. I never attended Mutual.

Time went on, yet those same four girls never gave up. They took a special interest in me. They always said "hi" at school and would stop and talk to me. They sat by me in classes. They found out which subjects I was flunking (due mostly to lack of study) and would invite themselves over to study with me.

I could not understand it. Why me? They knew the things I did—my reputation. Surely they felt my resentment toward them. Why did they keep on trying? I knew I was a lost cause. I felt pushed and cornered, my own conscience hurting. Still I fought them.

December 12 was my birthday. My family never made birthdays special. I got a "happy birthday" from my mom and nothing from my dad, and I went through the school day not letting anyone know I was a year older. I planned on celebrating that night by sneaking out and going over to see some friends.

At 8:00 that night the doorbell rang. I answered it and there stood my Mutual class. One girl had a cake in her hands and another a gallon of ice cream. They were all smiling and suddenly broke out singing "Happy Birthday." I didn't even know how to react.

I went to Mutual twice that month and once in January. But that was all. The three times I attended were great, and I felt a strange closeness toward those four girls, but the social pressure from my other friends was too great and after leading the kind of life I led all week, I just couldn't face those Mutual girls. Still they befriended me and never judged.

March 12 was a very dreary day in my life. I came home from school late. I had flunked an exam that afternoon and was very blue. I came home to find my parents in a very heated argument. Knowing how it would be, I went to my room and sat there, numb, just listening. I don't remember much after that except losing all control.

A few days later I gained consciousness in the hospital. For three weeks I lay in the hospital, and for three weeks not one of my friends came to see me. Not one! The very friends I had always gotten kicks with. Where were they now when I needed their friendship?

Instead, every day at 3:30 one of those four Mutual girls would be at my side. They were there every day. They brought me things to read, they sneaked in candy, and they brought in a transistor radio for me to listen to. We would do crossword puzzles together, and they would tell me the latest happenings at school. They never asked what happened and I never offered to tell.

After I got out of the hospital I began to go to Mutual. I finally realized that those four girls who had taken an interest in me really were sincere. Not only had I grown to like them, but now I felt a bond of love between us. My life seemed to be going so much better. I was happier than I had ever been.

April 2 was a day I shall never forget. It was a cold, dark, rainy day, a depressing day. During the final period of school, the principal walked into the room with a note for me. I was to go home immediately. "What now?" was my only thought. I grabbed my books and sweater and ran out.

It was pouring rain. I was glad I only lived four blocks from school, and yet with each block I felt a greater and greater despair. What was wrong at home?

By the time I reached the house I knew something dreadful had happened. I raced through the front door and almost collided head-on with my dad. I looked up into a ghostly white, tear-streaked face, a face I had never seen before. He was trembling all over and could only mutter, "She's gone, your mother's passed away."

Oh, how I loved her! I was stunned. I turned and I began to run. I ran and ran and my tears mixed with the rain. I ran until I was exhausted, but I did not stop. My face was swollen and my head hurt. Still I ran. Then, suddenly, I saw from the opposite direction someone coming toward me. I paused and wiped my eyes. Could it be? One of those four Mutual girls, the girls who truly cared about me? One of those girls was running through the rain for me. I began to run again, and when we met I threw my arms around that girl and we both collapsed to the ground. I sat there crying, and she cried with me.

In the years that followed, I became one with those four Mutual girls. I learned to care, really care about others and to give of myself. I found that by helping others my own problems diminished.

When the most important day of my life came, I knelt across the altar from my sweetheart and in the reflection of mirrors were those four Mutual girls, standing, with tears running down their cheeks. They had made this possible for me.

I'll never know why I had been so important to them. Me, a nobody. I can only thank my Father in heaven for those girls and pray with all my heart that there are many more like them in his Church.

Slightly modified from Yorgason and Yorgason, *Others*, 1–4.

He only is saved who endureth unto the end.

D&C 53:7

"THEY'RE MY LITTLE SWEETIES"
JOSEPH C. ANDREWS

When our bishopric prayerfully considered who to call for our new Sunbeam teacher in Primary, we were very surprised at the name that kept coming to us: Sister Garner. Sister Garner must have been eighty years old. She had raised a family of ten children; the oldest of her children was nearly sixty herself. Even her grandchildren were all married and gone from their homes. She had many great-grandchildren who were older than Sunbeams. Her husband was a faithful high priest—but his health had deteriorated to the point that he was totally unable to attend church. And now we felt we should call her to teach three-year-olds in Primary.

As bishop, I invited her to meet with me and the counselor over Primary. I didn't want to simply issue a calling; I wanted us to carefully explore how she was doing and how she would feel about such a calling. When we told her what we had in mind, she responded without hesitation. "I love little children. I'd love to do it."

"We're concerned about your health, and the health of your

husband," I said. "Even though we feel good spiritually about issuing this call, we also want to make sure you feel good about it. Would you like some time to think it over, to go home and pray about it?"

"No, I already feel good about it. This calling will be a blessing to me."

In our ward we had quite a number of older members. We didn't have enough younger people to staff the ward, so we often had to look among the elderly. But most of them had a stock, ready answer: "I've already had my turn at serving in the Primary (or Young Women or Young Men or Sunday School). You'll need to call someone else."

Not Sister Garner. She was ready and willing to do whatever we asked. And then she served with diligence.

That was her approach to teaching the Sunbeams in our ward. She understood little children and prepared meaningful lessons appropriate to their age. She held the children on her lap. She gave them hugs. She loved them. And she taught them about Heavenly Father and Jesus Christ and being a "Sunbeam for him." The little children looked forward to going to Primary, so they could see Sister Garner. They respected her and they loved her.

She was there every week, without fail, fulfilling her calling. She served through headaches, body aches, arthritis, fatigue, and the general pains and discomforts of old age. One day one of the other sisters said to her, "How can you bear spending two hours with all those noisy little kids?" Sister Garner answered, "They're not noisy little kids. They're my little sweeties."

After Sister Garner had served for two years, she came to me very concerned. "My hearing is failing," she said. "I can't hear the little children well enough to teach them."

"Do you want us to consider a release?" I asked her.

"No. I don't think so. But would you think about calling an assistant to help me?"

We did so, a young woman in her early twenties. They made a perfect pair, Sister Neld and Sister Garner. They served together for a year; then Sister Garner's health declined and we knew it was time to release her. She had served faithfully for the whole time she had been called, never tiring, never asking to quit, never giving less than 100 percent to the children she'd been called to bless—and all this in her old age.

*Stand as witnesses of God at all
times and in all things, and in all places.*

MOSIAH 18:9

TAXI TALK
JANET PETERSON

"I create opportunities for missionary work," states Bill Cortelyou, who has been a cab driver in a Boston suburb for twenty-two years. During the past fifteen years Brother Cortelyou has given away more than 6,000 copies of the Book of Mormon and 10,000 pamphlets of *The Prophet Joseph Smith's Testimony* to his passengers and other people he meets.

Brother Cortelyou files the material alphabetically by language and keeps them in a box in his cab or in an athletic bag that he carries when he uses public transportation. "Then when I meet an Ethiopian, for example, and ask if he speaks Amharic, I can quickly hand him the appropriate copy," says Brother Cortelyou. "I usually have something with me to give away. Otherwise, it is a lost opportunity."

Because Boston is a center for medicine, technology, finance, and education, people from all over the world gather there. Since Brother Cortelyou's route includes Logan International Airport, he transports visitors from places such as India, Nigeria,

Japan, Bolivia, and Italy. Among his passengers have been scientists, doctors, Nobel Prize winners, priests, rabbis, and government officials from many nations. He has given away copies of the Book of Mormon and Joseph Smith pamphlets in more than thirty-five languages, including Polish, Thai, Greek, Swahili, and Vietnamese. "Rarely do I encounter somebody who speaks a language that I don't have something for," he says.

On an average day Bill makes twenty trips in his cab. He typically gives Joseph Smith pamphlets or copies of the Book of Mormon to four or five of his passengers. "People don't often turn down my offer, because the Spirit helps me," he says. "They're usually very kind and receptive. Sometimes my offer leads to a discussion about the Church.

"I know of one person who has been baptized from my giving her a Book of Mormon. I would love to know about others, but when we give service we do not always know the outcome. My missionary work is to create opportunities for someone to make the choice about learning the truth of the gospel."

Brother Cortelyou grew up on Long Island, New York, and joined the Church while in his thirties. Though he did not have the opportunity to serve a full-time mission, missionary work is now one of the great joys of his life.

Slightly modified from Janet Peterson, "Taxi Talk," © by Intellectual Reserve, Inc. Previously published in the *Ensign*, Jan. 1998, 68–69.

The just man walketh in his integrity.

PROVERBS 20:7

"WHERE ARE THE OTHER GUYS?"
MATTHEW E. CHRISTENSEN

When Wayne Mills was sixteen, he left home for three months to work at Camp Billy Rice, a Boy Scout camp located some three hours north of Boise, Idaho. Billy Rice was situated next to Warm Lake, so named because of its favorable temperature. Wayne was one of several camp counselors who helped the youth earn merit badges and rank advancements. The counselors worked Monday through Friday, then had Saturday and Sunday off to relax, recreate, and worship.

Wayne served on the lake's waterfront, teaching younger Scouts to exercise responsibility in the water as they played or participated in various water sports. He also taught and assisted the boys in earning four merit badges—Canoeing, Rowing, Swimming, and Lifesaving.

On Saturdays, Wayne played chess with his friends, enjoyed water games in the lake, or went canoeing, rowing, swimming, or hiking. Sometimes they hiked or canoed to a lodge located across Warm Lake. They bought sodas or candy at the lodge and enjoyed the freedom of getting away from camp for awhile. Once or twice Wayne and his friends found and picked wild goose-berries and encouraged the camp's chief cook to prepare and bake gooseberry pies. And sometimes they traveled to Cascade, Idaho, a nearby resort town, where they sought entertainment, enjoyed fast food, and purchased needed supplies.

One Saturday Wayne and his friends drove to Cascade. They bought refreshments, walked around, played a game of billiards with some local teenagers, and ate lunch. Then the group decided to check out and possibly watch a matinee movie. They walked to the theater and saw that a movie rated PG-13 was playing. "Look what's on!" one of the boys exclaimed. "I've been wanting to see that." The others agreed.

But Wayne had heard about that particular movie. It had crude language and inappropriate scenes. "You guys go ahead if you like," Wayne said. "I think I'll pass." He didn't make a big deal of it, but he wasn't about to lower his standards for that movie.

Wayne knew that his parents or bishop would never find out if he saw the movie. They were back home, far away. Besides, it wasn't even rated R. His parents, however, had taught him well. He had been blessed by family home evening lessons, scripture readings, and many family prayers that served to teach him right from wrong. And besides, he held the office of priest in the Aaronic Priesthood and knew that priests should not be watching that kind of entertainment.

The friends went into the theater and Wayne began walking down Cascade's main street, wondering what to do with himself for the next two hours. Minutes later, Billy Rice's camp director, Marvin Laub, drove into town and spotted Wayne walking alone. Mr. Laub knew that Wayne had originally gone to town with a group. He pulled his vehicle over. "Where are the other guys? Why are you alone?" Wayne hesitated. He didn't want to cast his friends in a bad light. But as he considered it, he decided to share with Mr. Laub, also a member of the Church, his decision not to watch that particular movie.

Mr. Laub was pleased. "Wayne, it took real courage to make the proper decision—even though it left you alone in town with nothing to do. And I know that your friends might try to make fun of you later. Don't let them get to you. I'm really proud of you and of the fine young man you are choosing to be even when your parents may never know of your decision."

Mr. Laub drove on his way. But he was so impressed with Wayne's choices that he later contacted Wayne's parents. "I just want you to know what a wonderful boy you're raising," he said. "Let me tell you about the day I saw him walking alone in a little town in the mountains. . . ."

A bishop must be blameless, as the steward of God.

TITUS 1:7

HIS LIGHT IN MY LIFE
MARION D. HANKS

I was twelve years old and a Tenderfoot Scout when I experienced my first overnight excursion away from home. I was excited, and I was frightened; we all were.

The group of boys who lined up with their gear on the lawn of the old 19th Ward building in Salt Lake City were variously equipped for the planned adventure to Lake Blanche in the high mountains to the east of us. Some had elaborate and expensive sleeping bags and pack frames, and some had bedrolls attached to old army knapsacks. I was in between, having the use of a home-made bag fashioned by my brother-in-law, together with the pack frame he had built, on which the bag and contents would be lashed.

All of us had been told to lay out our equipment for inspection by the man in charge, and we each fearfully waited by our stuff as the examiner approached. No marine trainee facing his sergeant could have been more apprehensive.

The man passed down the line rather quickly, commenting on this item or that boy's pack, directing the abandonment of this extra baggage, sending one boy home to his mother with the three clean sheets she had sent along for his big trip.

I was last in line and thus nearest home, since our little house lay just alongside the old Relief Society building that separated us from the chapel. There was a narrow alley between the chapel and that building, and at the end of it a wall which formed the east border of our yard.

Being closest to home might have been an indicator of my frame of mind, because I was not altogether sold on this adventure and I was a bit apprehensive about the equipment I had borrowed, having been admonished carefully to keep it very clean and in absolute good repair.

When the inspector reached me, many foolish questions had been asked and answered, with increasing impatience, I suspect, so that the man as he faced me had become a bit short on good will. He was, in fact, quite a dynamic person of whom I was somewhat afraid, though he had always been appropriately dignified in his calling and never had been anything but kind to me.

This day under the circumstances and with the provocation of so much juvenile incompetency, he reached the end of his rope. Observing the number of items I was carrying, which seemed to him superfluous for the high mountains and which he felt should not be carried in my pack, he sternly directed me to remove them and take them home to my mother. He seemed to dwell a bit sarcastically upon the pronunciation of my first name, about which my life on the west side of town by the railroad tracks had made me a bit touchy, if not defensive.

When he seemed to be making fun of me, the other boys up the line, having had their turn, snickered or broke into open laughter. Everybody but I thought it was funny. When he had left me and returned up the line to begin to herd the crowd onto the trucks which were to transport us, I made my gesture of protest. Not having anything else to do that I could think of, I just bent over, picked up the pack frame in one hand, and the two ends of the sleeping bag on which my gear was resting in the other, and walked up the alley, dragging it all behind me. When I reached the wall I dropped over, retrieved the equipment, and dragged it all behind the coal shed which was separated by a few feet from our house. Then I sat down on the ground under the basketball hoop on the back of the coal shed and suffered the pains and anguish of the damned—that is, those who have through willfulness and stubbornness painted themselves into an impossible position. I was twelve years old and in trouble.

I could not retreat and keep my self-respect; this man of authority had made a fool of me in front of others and had, to me quite unjustifiably, subjected me to ridicule. I was resentful and hopelessly frustrated. I could not see a way out of my dilemma, and I was deeply distressed.

After a long time—no doubt it seemed much longer than it actually was, but it was a long time—I heard footsteps coming up our pathway from the front street, heard the pause and a murmured conversation at our back door, and then felt and heard him resume his pace toward me. Mother had told him where I was.

He came down the little passageway between our house and

the coal shed, around the corner, and sat down beside me on the dirt. He said nothing for a time but joined me as I nervously flipped little rocks and clods of dirt with a stick between my feet. I didn't look at him. After a time he spoke.

"Do you ever get up on Kotter's garage?" "Does Brother Kotter care?" "Do walnuts from the Perkinses' tree fall in your backyard?" "If you take ten shots at this hoop from the line over there, how many can you make?"

I gave brief answers to all questions, and again there was silence.

Then a large, strong hand reached over to my knee and grasped it warmly.

"Son," he said, "I made a mistake and I'm sorry."

"That's all right, Bishop," I said.

"Are you ready to go now," he said. "The others are waiting."

"Okay," I said.

"We better get your pack ready."

He helped me roll the gear into the sleeping bag, secure it to the pack frame, and lift it to my back. We then walked out past our back door to the street and onto the truck where the others were waiting. I later learned that after I had left he had called all of them together and explained that he had made a mistake and had been unkind to me and that my reaction had been understandable. He apologized to them in my behalf, prepared them to receive me without clamor when I arrived, got them all ready in the truck, and then made the long walk back to find me.

I do not dramatize what might have happened had a good

man who was also a great man and a generous man not made that long walk, if he had not been mature enough and humble enough and capable of acknowledging and correcting a mistake. I know I was wounded and frustrated by the impossibility of my circumstance. I know that he was the bishop we prayed for by name at our house every day. And I know that my wonderful mother who did not intrude on my dilemma must have helped pray him up the path.

I also know that boys and girls, even stubborn and rebellious ones, or hurt ones or bewildered ones, are worth something to our Heavenly Father and should be worth something to all the rest of his children. I do know that I myself have taken a few long walks when my own sense of pride or impatience might have prevailed, whispering to me, "Ah, let him go. Let him sit there and see how he likes it. Why should I be bothered?"

To this hour I remain grateful that my wonderful bishop overcame any such thoughts, if he had them, and made that long walk.

His light in my life has made a difference.

From Hanks, "His Light in My Life," *New Era*, Nov. 1984, 4–6.

Remember the sabbath day, to keep it holy.

EXODUS 20:8

THE BETTER CHOICE
JANE BELDON

When my son Barry was sixteen years old, he was thrilled to finally have his driver's license. But that happiness was jarred considerably one day when he borrowed his sister's car and put a new dent in her car door.

His happiness was further compromised when he was informed he would have to pay to have the dent fixed.

So Barry got a job at a local fast-food place. His boss told him that he would have to work on Sundays. "That's okay," he said to himself. "I really need the job. It won't be so bad to work on Sundays."

When he came home and told me that he had a new job I was proud of him. Then he told me that he would have to work on Sundays. We talked about the importance of keeping the Sabbath day holy. Yes, some people have vital jobs that might require them to work on Sundays, such as doctors or firemen. But did a job in a fast-food restaurant qualify?

Barry pondered and prayed about our talk, made his decision, and went to work. During his shift he told his boss. "I've decided I don't want to work on Sundays."

The boss tried to change his mind. "Oh, come on, Barry. It's not that big a deal. If your Sabbath is so important, then why do I see families in here after church buying ice cream for their kids? I'm not going to make an exception. Everyone who works here will have to take a turn at working on Sunday."

Barry shook his head and said politely, "I want to work here. I need the money. But don't count on me for Sundays." For a time all went well. Then one day the manager put Barry's name on the Sunday schedule. When Barry saw that, he approached the boss. He felt like he was shaking with fear, but he knew he had to do it. "Mr. Johnson. I'm sorry, but I won't be here this Sunday. I'm scheduled for it, but I can't come."

The following Monday Barry showed up for work on time. His boss was waiting. "Barry, this isn't working out. I told you that you had to work yesterday, and you shrugged it off." Barry tried to talk to him about it, but the boss was too upset. "Listen, it's simple," he said. "If you're not willing to work on Sundays, then you might as well find some other place to work."

Feeling he knew better, Barry quit. He had decided that that job was not worth offending God over. Interestingly, during the weeks he did work there, he earned precisely the amount of money he needed to pay for the repair on his sister's car.

He commanded them that they should
observe the sabbath day, and keep it holy.

MOSIAH 18:23

A NOBLE EFFORT
JANET THOMAS

Rachelle Noble did not have to face the problem of playing on Sundays until she was a freshman in college. She remembers the day perfectly. She was in her first year at Columbia University in New York City. She had been recruited to be a member of Columbia's track-and-field team, to participate in the throwing events. She had told her coach up front that she would not be participating in Sunday meets.

"I was in my room," says Rachelle. "I had just received our media guide, and I was looking at the schedule. I saw that half of our season's meets were going to be on Sundays. At that moment, all the stories I had heard in Primary and all the lessons I had had in Sunday School came back to me. I had talked to my parents about it. That's when my decision became conscious. I would not be playing on Sundays."

That's when strange things started happening. Her first meet was switched to Saturday. Then weather caused another Sunday cancellation. Then the biggest meet was changed at the last minute. In the meets that were not rescheduled, Rachelle participated in events on Saturday but would then bow out on Sunday. Her coaches tried to persuade her to change her mind the whole year. At the end, Rachelle felt that she needed to play for a coaching staff she was more comfortable with.

Rachelle then transferred to a junior college near her hometown of Show Low, Arizona. The problem with Sunday competition went away since no junior college meets were scheduled for Sunday. But Rachelle wanted to pursue her talents at the highest levels of college competition, so she sent a highlight film and her transcript to a lot of schools, including UCLA. It was a long shot because the UCLA track team was among the best college teams in the nation, and the UCLA throwing coach didn't take transfer students.

Rachelle's dream started to come true. Coach Art Venegas at UCLA called and asked her to come. Then came the hard part. Rachelle says, "He was really excited and saying all this really cool stuff, and I decided that would be the time to tell him. I told him I can't compete on Sunday." Even if she had to give up her dream, Rachelle couldn't change her mind. But the coach said, "Okay, I don't see any problem with that."

Then the coach said something that let Rachelle know he was serious. "He said if they schedule the NCAA hammer throw, which is my best event, on Sunday, you just won't throw it."

Unfortunately, that's exactly what happened. The hammer throw was scheduled for Sunday in the big Pacific-10 Conference meet in Seattle. Rachelle was expected to win or place. Her performance could mean the difference in points between her team winning or losing the entire meet. An assistant coach asked her, out of curiosity, why she had made this stand. "I told him," says Rachelle, "that even if I won on Sunday, I would have this piece of metal, but I would have gone against everything I've learned for the last eighteen years. It made total sense to him."

It turned out that her team didn't need the points Rachelle might have earned. The team took first in the meet.

Rachelle feels that blessings have come from her decision. On that Sunday afternoon, after the big Pac-10 meet, Rachelle's coach approached where she was sitting in her Sunday dress waiting for the team bus. He handed her his coaching credentials as a souvenir and said, "I want you to have this. You've given me the most memorable performance of this meet."

Editor's note: Since this story was written, Rachelle Noble won the Pac-10 track-and-field meet in the hammer throw, setting a meet record. The organizing committee had voted to change the event from Sunday to Saturday so Rachelle could participate. Rachelle has been called to serve in the Lithuania Vilnius Mission.

Janet Thomas, "Noble Effort," © by Intellectual Reserve, Inc. Previously published in the *New Era*, Oct. 1998, 12–14.

And he who feeds you, or clothes you,
or gives you money, shall in nowise lose his reward.

D&C 84:90

MY UNEXPECTED HEROES
John M. Wells

For as long as I can remember, I have wanted to own my own business. For years I worked as a candy salesman, delivering to grocery stores in my region of the state, and I took every opportunity to talk to the grocers about their business. I wanted to learn what worked and what didn't, hoping that someday I would have my own store.

Finally the opportunity came. With much help from a bank, I was able to purchase a small grocery store in a nearby town. It was a frightening thing to quit my job and move my family, but it was also thrilling to be able to fulfill my long-held dream.

Unfortunately, we started deeply in debt and quickly saw the hole get deeper. As the years passed, I was forced to make a decision: either go out of business, or keep the store alive with a series of short-term loans. I chose to keep the store alive.

The story of how we were able to meet those loan payments, which often seemed to come at the most inopportune of times, is a story of true miracles and blessings. It is a story of the blessing of paying a full and honest tithe even when you don't have money left over to pay your bills. I saw over and over again how the Lord keeps his promises to his children who keep theirs.

After we'd had the store for nearly a decade, we had an experience I'll never forget, an experience that introduced me to some unexpected heroes. I was serving in a stake presidency at the time. One week a bank note came due for $10,000. I had to come up with the money or literally lose all we'd worked and sacrificed for for so long. But the problem was that I had no way in the world to come up with that money.

I felt I should confide in my stake president, just so he'd be aware of the stress and difficulty his counselor was working under—and because I welcomed his faith and prayers in my behalf. I outlined for him the background of the problem, explaining how I had been forced to work on the basis of short-term loans for many years, and how the Lord had often rescued me at the last moment.

"I don't know what his will is for me this time," I said. "It kind of feels like I might be at the end of my rope. I just wanted you to know that your counselor might be out beating the bushes for work next week, if I'm not able to resolve this somehow."

He thanked me for confiding in him and told me he'd join his faith and prayers to mine. I was comforted, but still didn't have any idea of how I'd be able to come up with the money.

A couple of days later President Wright called me on the

phone. "We're having a special presidency meeting this Sunday, a half hour before high council meeting. I've got some things I need us to discuss. Can you come?" Of course I could.

The following Sunday morning, at a very early hour, I entered the stake presidency's office. There was the stake president and my fellow counselor in the presidency. I was also surprised to see three high councilors there. President Wright stood and shook my hand, then gestured for me to sit.

"President Wells," he said, addressing me, "I hope you don't mind, but I took the liberty of sharing your financial dilemma with these brethren. They have all received it in the utmost confidence. Now here's what I propose we do. These men aren't rich, as you know. But the Lord has blessed them. Because we all love you, we each wish to give you $2,000 to help you repay your loan."

I was astounded. "President, I didn't share this with you so that you'd offer me money!" I said.

"Of course not. But you need the money and we need to share. Pay us back when you can. But I don't believe the Lord wants you to lose your store. You need it and your family needs it."

I was overwhelmed with gratitude, and my feelings ran close to the surface. Giving me that money would be a true sacrifice for some of those men. Two thousand dollars back then would almost buy a new car. You could buy a nice home for $20,000. And these, my brothers in the priesthood, were giving me that money with no strings attached—just "pay us back when you can."

I was able to pay them back, with interest. But in the meantime, my unexpected heroes saved my livelihood and enabled me to continue operating my grocery store for many years to come.

Remember the worth of souls is great in the sight of God.

D&C 18:10

A DIFFERENT DRUMMER
LISA PRALL

On October of 1992, a new freshman without much enthusiasm for life arrived at Page (Arizona) High School. Darryle had spent the previous several years in a boarding school for the handicapped. He was confined to a wheelchair because of cerebral palsy; he had no ability to speak, see, or walk; and he had limited use of his arms. When he first arrived, he was very scared, and nobody seemed to know how to help him.

As teachers we were becoming quite frustrated trying to find something that would capture his interest. Things changed when someone brought in a tape of Navajo drum music. That perked Darryle up. He loved this music, and we knew we had to capitalize on this.

It was arranged for Darryle to attend the band class, something he seemed to enjoy. I, too, was excited for him, but I knew I had the personnel to take Darryle to the class only once a week.

Enter Brad Ross. Brad was a quiet, shy sophomore with a great love for music. The next afternoon, about the time band class began, Brad walked into my special education classroom. He was very quiet, and I could tell he was nervous. But that didn't stop him. He marched up to me and asked if he could take Darryle to band with him.

I was stunned. I let Brad take Darryle, but I remember thinking that it wouldn't last.

What followed was the most honest expression of heroism I have ever witnessed. For the next three years, Brad never missed a day. Each day he would come to my classroom and escort Darryle to band practice. Darryle became as much a part of the band as any other member. Every day, Brad would set Darryle up with different percussion instruments. With eager delight, Darryle would sense the music and gleefully join in the rhythms he felt. Under Brad's patient tutoring, Darryle learned to play the snare drum, bass drum, tambourine, maracas, and the triangle. Even though Darryle's rhythms did not always match the rest of the band's, Darryle was totally involved.

The things Brad did were thoughtful actions that required discipline and sacrifice. His heroic efforts affected the other students and touched the hearts of many teachers and parents. He had the bravery necessary to walk into a classroom full of special education students, make friends with someone who needed a friend, create a new program for a peer, and provide the selfless service necessary to see it through.

Lisa Prall, "A Different Drummer," © by Intellectual Reserve, Inc. Previously published in the *New Era*, Sept. 1998, 49.

For after much tribulation come the blessings.
Wherefore the day cometh that ye shall be crowned with much glory;
the hour is not yet, but is nigh at hand.

D&C 58:4

HE RODE HIS BIKE TO CHURCH
TRISHA COFFMAN

Recently there was a story in the news about a young boy who called 911 when he found his mother unconscious on their kitchen floor. He had learned—perhaps in school, maybe from his parents—that calling 911 was the right thing to do in an emergency, and because he remembered that instruction and acted on it, his mother's life was saved, and he was deemed a hero.

Another child hero is a boy named Marcus, someone who had learned at a tender age another way to call for help in emergencies, whether spiritual or temporal. He was just three years old when LDS missionaries knocked on his family's door. His older brother, who was eighteen, became interested in the Church, decided to be baptized, and began taking Marcus to church with him every Sunday. A couple of years later the brother married and moved away, but Marcus still attended church on his own, eager to learn all that he was being taught in Primary about a Heavenly Father and his Son, Jesus Christ.

One night, five-year-old Marcus woke up in the middle of the night, overcome by horrible feelings. He struggled, but felt unable to move and found it impossible to go back to sleep. He was very afraid, but recalling the things he had learned in church concerning prayer, Marcus prayed, closing in the name of Jesus Christ, as he'd been taught. The instant he said those words aloud, the fearful feelings that had paralyzed him fled.

This was Marcus's first experience with testimony and the strength of the Spirit. That night, by calling out in prayer, he gained a testimony of the power of prayer. He knew then of a surety that he had a Heavenly Father who was real and who loved him, that Christ was real, and that Jesus' name was sacred and held immense and marvelous power.

It was this first testimony that urged Marcus to church every week on his own. In attending all by himself as he did, he showed himself to be another kind of hero. He was only kindergarten age, but he rode his bike to church each Sunday because he knew that was what Heavenly Father wanted him to do. Week after week he went—getting himself ready, going out to his bike, and riding off to the church by himself, never missing, never failing.

When Marcus turned eight, he wanted to be baptized. He pleaded repeatedly with his mother to allow him to join the Church, but she steadfastly refused to give him permission.

A few years later he finally stopped attending his meetings and made some new friends who didn't encourage him in good choices. But soon Marcus decided he missed having the gospel as a part of his life and returned to church. Again he had no support from home. Again he got himself up, ready, and out of the house. Again he rode his bike to church faithfully, week after week, never missing. Finally his mom realized the effect for good the church was having on her son, and around his thirteenth birthday she agreed at last to let him be baptized.

The night of his baptism, Marcus once again climbed on his bike, now a white ten-speed, to ride to the church. As always before, it was his own responsibility to get himself to the meetinghouse. It was a rainy Saturday night in the summer, and as Marcus rode in the storm, he was suddenly hit by a car and thrown from his bike. He strongly felt that something evil was trying to keep him from joining the Church—the same source of opposition that had succeeded in keeping him from baptism for the previous five years. With no apparent injuries, he jumped back on his now-bent bicycle and continued on to the church. There he saw an entire chapel filled with supportive ward members, all there for Marcus, who had been coming to church on his own for so many years.

Throughout his life, Marcus has remembered the night when, as a small boy, he was able, through prayer, to chase away the feelings of fear that had awakened him, an experience he feels was meant to keep him away from the gospel. Instead, the experience gave him a testimony and a lifelong dedication to pursuing the work of his Heavenly Father.

Take no thought for your life, what ye shall
eat, or what ye shall drink; nor yet for your body, what
ye shall put on. . . . But seek ye first the kingdom of God, and his
righteousness; and all these things shall be added unto you.

MATTHEW 6:25, 33

THE LEAST AMONG US
WAYNE B. LYNN

Our small, rented Volkswagen had carried us deep into the interior of central Mexico. We bumped along on this fascinating journey over winding dirt roads through small villages and past clusters of farm homes. Now, as it grew dark, the homes could be seen only by their flickering lights. It was Sunday night and the hour was growing late. The heat of the afternoon lingered in the quiet summer air. We trusted our friend, who was driving and who had lived here before, to find the Church members' home. We had asked him to help us get to know some of the members and to learn more about the country.

A cloud of dust followed us when we finally pulled up beside a tall adobe fence surrounding a dwelling. Our car lights shined on two large metal gates hanging on sturdy hinges. The gates met in the center of the gateway where they were held together with a heavy chain and padlock. We watched in the car lights as our friend, who had been driving, walked to the gate and pounded his fist against the heavy metal. In a few moments the chain was unlocked from the inside, and a short man with a dark complexion opened the gate. He was dressed in black pants, a white short-sleeved shirt, and a black tie. After a moment's pause there was recognition, followed by a wide, spontaneous smile and embrace.

We were soon introduced to him, and he invited us into his home. As we walked through the courtyard toward the small, humble dwelling, I noted that a new, more commodious home was under construction nearby. We were greeted at the door by a gracious wife. She too was small in stature. Her raven hair hung in long braids, and her dark eyes sparkled as she smiled and bade us welcome. She was a beautiful, quiet woman, her countenance clearly depicting her Lamanite heritage. The room we entered was virtually half of their home. It served as kitchen, dining room, and bedroom. We were invited to sit on the edge of the bed. Our hostess soon presented each of us with a slice of watermelon. It was a welcome, delicious treat to our thirsty bodies. As we ate I noticed our host had not joined with us and inquired why. I was told that he had just returned from a home teaching visit. The family he had visited was facing some challenges, so he was fasting and praying in their behalf. Our conversation turned to his new home and their progress on its construction. We learned that work on the home had been postponed for the past year because their financial resources and time were directed toward helping build their branch building that had just been completed.

"I guess now that the chapel is finished you will be able to start working on your house?"

"No. You see, a young man in our branch wants to go on a mission, and we will all be helping finance him. Our home will have to wait."

I glanced around at the humble surroundings. Tears came to my eyes. A small closet held the limited wardrobe for husband and wife. I saw a clean but painfully modest home with no running water, no carpeted floors or soft sofas with matching drapes, no TV or refrigerator, no sink or dishwasher—a home poor in worldly possessions but rich in spirit, a home filled with love, sanctified by devotion and sacrifice.

One day, I thought to myself, *I will want to gain admittance through another gate into the celestial realms on high. I think I will just slip my thumb into the corner of this man's pocket and let him pull me along. When we approach the gate, I will smile at the gatekeeper and say, "I'm with him."*

Lynn, *Lessons from Life,* 59–61.

Her children arise up, and call her blessed.

PROVERBS 31:28

"IF I CAN JUST BE LIKE MY MOM"
ELISABETH S. CHILD

From my earliest memory I knew that my mother was special. But it wasn't until I was older that I understood how truly extraordinary she is.

Even when she was a little girl, my mom wanted to have a big family, and she did. She thought being a loving and righteous mother was the greatest dream any girl could have. She has held prominent positions in the ward and stake. But truly, to her the most important calling has been that of *mother*.

In addition, her heart was big enough to hold many other children as well. My parents invited many foster children into our home, having them for more than twenty years.

When my parents were building their home, one of Mom's main goals was to have a house her children would want to stay in, instead of going off to play at the neighbors. So they built a home with a big playroom. She also had the house built so that no matter where she was in the house, she could easily look into the playroom and see the kids. I know some mothers who cheer when their children leave to go play. But my mom enjoyed her children so much she wanted them to be around her.

Our house became the neighborhood hangout for kids of all ages. Many were our close friends; others were kids who simply needed a loving place to be. I can't tell you how many kids have told me my mom was their "second mom" and what a blessing she was (and is) in their lives.

When I was in grade school, Mom was very sick for a long time, and she had to spend much of her time in bed. But that didn't stop her from loving us. "Be sure to come see me when you get home from school," she would say. After school we would each take a turn by her bedside, telling her about our day, getting hugs, and being blessed by her smiles. Even though she was sick, she would find ways to serve and bless us, even if all she had to offer was the sound of a loving voice.

When summer vacations came, Mom would rejoice. "Now I get you for the whole summer," she'd say. "Three whole months!" When school started in the fall again, she was sorry that we'd be gone for so long each day. "I'll miss you today," she would say. "Always remember I love you."

I loved to talk to my mom. She never got tired of listening to me. Once in awhile I would say, "I'm sorry, Mom, I'm just babbling." She would answer, "I like it."

One of the remarkable things about Mom was her spiritual strength. I remember one time she went to general conference by herself. My dad was busy working that day, but she still wanted to go. This was back in the days when a person had to get in line very early in the morning and wait to even have a chance of getting into the Tabernacle. The week after conference she shared her experience with us in a special family night.

She told us that after a very long wait, she made it into the Tabernacle for the first session of the day. The Spirit was so strong and the experience so wonderful that as soon as that session was over she ran back to the end of the line, hoping to attend the second session as well. As the ushers started to seat people for the second session, my mom watched as the line advanced, hoping she could make it in. She got closer and closer to the door—then, not far ahead of her, they stopped the line. The Tabernacle was full. Her heart sank. Then the ushers asked people to squeeze closer together on the benches. They let in a few more people. Mom was literally the last person in.

As she told the story, I was touched by how important it was to her to be able to attend conference, to be able to see and hear the prophet of the Lord in person. I was touched by the depth of her gratitude as she told about being able to enter the Tabernacle doors. Some people had traveled thousands of miles to attend. Mom had traveled only a dozen. Yet her feelings of gratitude and joy seemed to be just as great as if she had had to make a great sacrifice to be there.

As a teenager I felt a burning desire to do the right thing. I would often get frustrated with myself for my mistakes and inadequacies. I would often say to myself, "If I can just be like my mom, then I will be okay." I was right. I have always strived to be like her because I know she is the best example in my life of how to be a Christlike person.

One night when I was seventeen and a senior in high school, I was alone in my room when my mom came in. She told me she felt impressed to encourage me to bring the Lord and his Spirit more fully into my life. She explained that it wasn't enough just to be active in the Church, that we needed to truly give our hearts to God. I felt excited, nervous, and honored. I wanted to do it, but I did not know exactly how to proceed. She told me to pray and promised that Heavenly Father would help me know exactly what to do. "If you get stuck," she said, "come and see me. We can talk some more."

She went downstairs to bed. I stayed in my room and prayed. It wasn't too long before I was in my parents' room asking Mom for help because I was stuck!

About this time I had several invitations to go on a trip after my graduation from high school. The choir was going to California, the dance classes were going on a cruise, the drama department was organizing a trip to New York, and some friends were thinking of taking a trip somewhere fun. It seemed to be an important enough decision that I should make it a matter for pondering and prayer. But as I carefully considered my choices, I felt stumped. Finally I went to my mom for help. We talked through the possibilities and then prayed together. Gradually an understanding came from the Spirit: Heavenly Father did not want me to go on *any* of those trips. Instead, he wanted me to spend some special time with my mom, seeking to further grow in my understanding of things of the Spirit.

The summer after I graduated, my mom and I set aside a few days to go on a little trip together. We didn't go to any fancy restaurants, amusement parks, exotic locations, or recreational places. We just went to a quiet place where we could be alone. While we were there we studied, prayed, and talked. I asked my mom gospel questions, and she answered them. She also taught me about subjects that she felt inspired to discuss. That time with my mom was one of the most precious experiences of my life. We grew closer together and closer to our Father in Heaven.

My spiritual learning from my mom did not end with that trip. Days, weeks, months, and even years later we would seek each other out for teaching, learning, and growing together. Even now, though I have a family and a home of my own, I still turn to my mom to teach me about spiritual things.

My mother has been not only a physical mother to me. She has been something far greater. She has been my spiritual mother—meaning that she nurtured, cared for, and loved me in my spiritual needs just as good mothers nurture, care for, and love their children in their physical and emotional needs. I will always honor and love her. I am so grateful for what she has taught me and for the sweet relationship we share.

Walk . . . with longsuffering, forbearing one another in love.

EPHESIANS 4:1–2

"I DIDN'T ASK THEM TO COME"
ATWELL J. PARRY

When I was growing up, my father didn't seem to have much use for the Church. I can never remember my dad going to church with me—not once. My mother made sure that I went to Primary and to Sunday meetings, but most of the time my brother and I went alone or with the neighbors.

Dad's attitude and lack of commitment continued in the decades that followed. When I was called to be bishop, I invited my folks to attend the sacrament meeting where I was to be sustained, telling them that something important was going to take place. My mother came, but Dad wouldn't. When Mom returned home and told him that I was the new bishop, Dad said, "Doesn't the kid have enough to do already?"

Many times when the home teachers would drop by and Dad would be downstairs working in his shop—where he worked on his hobbies, fine woodworking and rock cutting—Mom would go to the stairwell and call down, "Atwell, the home teachers are here." Dad would respond very loudly, "I didn't ask them to come"—which was always embarrassing for Mom, to say the least.

In fact, most of the time when the subject of "church" came up it developed into a difficult time for her.

I don't think it would be much of an exaggeration to say that Dad was a very hard case. But then four heroes changed everything.

When my dad was in his early sixties, the Church was building a new stake center in his area. A good brother in the ward asked Dad if he would be willing to help work on the new building. Of course, it didn't take Dad long to say, "No!" But after this brother left, Mom said to Dad, "If you don't do some work on that new church building, I will never again set foot in a Mormon church building of any kind." Dad didn't say anything at the time, and I have no idea how my mother must have felt. (I suspect she was bluffing, but she probably felt she was at the end of her rope on the church issue.) I also don't know where she got the courage to speak up like that, because my dad, though loving and kind, could also be quite gruff. But she did speak up and became the first hero in my Dad's story.

A few days later, a car pulled up in front of their home, and the driver honked the horn. Dad didn't say anything; he just got up from his chair, put on his old work coat, picked up his hammer, and started for the door.

"Where are you going?" Mom asked. Dad said, "I'm going to work on that blankety-blank building, so you can go to church."

That was the start of a new life for my father. He spent many weeks working with the men of the ward on the building. He got to know them and began to feel comfortable around them. One of those men was his home teacher. I'm sure that home teacher must have often wondered if he was making any headway with Dad. But as Dad worked on the building and became acquainted with those good Mormon brethren, including the home teacher, he no longer stayed downstairs when the home teachers visited. He actually welcomed them into his home. And he and the home teacher became friends. This faithful home teacher was the second hero, going out of his way to reach out to Dad, to love and bless him, to seek to befriend Dad even when Dad only wanted to rebuff him.

The third hero was a wise and caring bishop. The bishop had a family to care for, full-time employment, a ward to watch over, a stake center to help build—and he still found time to get to know my dad and to help him feel more comfortable with the Church. One of Dad's fears was that if he attended priesthood meeting, he would be asked to give a prayer or a talk. He insisted that those were things he just couldn't do. The bishop assured Dad that he would never be asked to pray or asked embarrassing questions. With those assurances, my dad began to attend sacrament meetings, with his home teacher friend sitting close by. Then my father took another leap and began to go to priesthood meetings! It took real courage for him to go back to church after fifty years of total inactivity. But he did. He is the fourth hero in his own story.

The bishop gave Dad the assignment to see that the rack holding tithing envelopes and donation slips was always full. He also asked Dad to come to priesthood meeting a little early to see that the hymn books were put on the chairs, and to stay a little after to pick them up. Dad fulfilled these assignments faithfully.

Dad had been ordained a priest as a young man but had never been advanced to the Melchizedek Priesthood. When it came time for him to be made an elder, I had the opportunity to lay my hands on my father's head and confer the Melchizedek Priesthood on him and ordain him. Shortly after that, Dad was asked to be the elders quorum secretary. He took to that assignment like a fish to water.

At that time I was serving as a counselor in the stake presidency. Dad's elders quorum presidency would hold their meeting in the same building and on the same night as the stake presidency. Once in awhile Dad and I would meet in the hallway. I was not used to seeing him in church, so when we met I wasn't sure how to greet him—a handshake, a hug, a nod as we passed? I finally decided that he would be most comfortable if I were to greet him as I did others—with a handshake.

One evening as I came out of the high council room, Dad was walking toward me down the hall. As he got close to me he put his arm around my shoulders and said, "Your mother and I are going to the Idaho Falls Temple in a couple of weeks. We would like you to go with us." Then with a twinkle in his eye he added, "If you think you can get a recommend."

My wife and I went to the Idaho Falls Temple with my mom and dad. After they were sealed as husband and wife, I had the incredible privilege of being sealed to them.

I was a little concerned about how Dad would receive the

temple ceremony, especially given his long-term inactivity and his long-standing fear of participating in any Church activity. But he accepted the temple ordinances and covenants immediately and developed a great love for the temple. He would take every opportunity to make the trip from Nampa, Idaho, to Idaho Falls to attend the temple.

Dad contracted cancer, and during the last few years of his life, he became very ill and was in a lot of pain. At that time, Dad had to give up his calling as elders quorum secretary, the only calling he had ever had. When he returned his record books, tears filled his eyes and flowed down his cheeks. It nearly broke his heart to give up the calling he loved so much. In spite of his illness, he continued to make as many trips to the temple as he could. The last trip he made was in the back of a station wagon. Ward members fixed up a bed for him so he could lie down most of the time traveling to Idaho Falls and back.

Because my mother was bold at just the right moment, because of a home teacher who wouldn't give up, because of a wise and caring bishop, and because my dad was willing to soften his heart toward the Church, I saw my mother's dreams and desires come true as she knelt at the altar in the temple to be sealed to my dad. My own hopes and wishes came true at the same moment. I have a great deal of love and gratitude for those brethren, who took so much time to befriend and love my father into the Church, for my mother for speaking up with courage, and for my father for responding, finally, with a humble heart.

Let us not be weary in well doing.

SHE SAW MY NEED
JENNA TREVORS

Soon after the birth of my fifth child, I bought a new home and was preparing to make the big move. I was very tired. I hardly had the energy to care for my children, let alone do all the other things that now faced me with the move to another home—unpacking, putting things in order, and even painting the outside of the house.

We finally got all of our possessions moved to the new house. As I sat in the living room holding my newborn daughter, surrounded by many boxes and feeling overwhelmed by all the work that was left to do, a knock sounded at my door. I opened the door and there stood Susan, one of my new neighbors, a woman who lived just down the street. She said, "I am here to help you." I couldn't believe she would be so concerned about me. She saw my circumstances but made no judgments. And she didn't *offer* to help—she just informed me that that's what she was going to do.

Susan showed up every day, cheerful, willing, and energetic. She stayed at least eight hours a day for many days, until everything in the house was put away. Then she continued to come for two more weeks to help me paint the outside of my house. I never called her to ask her to help. But each morning as I went out to start painting I would see her walking up the street in her "paint clothes." Through it all, we laughed, groaned under the load, and shared deep feelings with one another.

But that wasn't all she did. After a time Susan saw another need. She began to help me sort and organize all of my papers. Though the task was tedious and very time consuming, she helped me go through every paper I had. She showed me how to set up files and keep things in order. She also helped me organize everything else in my house, making it easier to care for and keep clean.

It wasn't that Susan was bored and had nothing to do. She had a busy home and six children of her own to care for. She just saw a need, and she and her family made sacrifices to fill that need.

I can't imagine how I would have survived those days without Susan. She was able to turn a huge trial into a blessing—and became my dear friend forever.

Wait on the Lord: be of good courage,
and he shall strengthen thine heart.

PSALM 27:14

COURAGE IN A MOVIE THEATER
DIANE BILLS PRINCE

Angie and her date arrived at the theater with the two other couples in their group. They found good seats inside and made themselves comfortable. Angie was having a great time until the movie began. Everything was all right for a while, but suddenly some scenes came up on the screen that made her feel extremely uncomfortable, scenes she knew she should not be polluting her life with. She turned to her date and whispered that the movie was making her uncomfortable and that she would wait in the lobby for him and the others. Then she had the additional courage to quietly get up and walk out by herself.

In the lobby, Angie was at peace inside. As embarrassing as it had been for her to get up and leave, she knew she had done the right thing.

Within a very short period of time, her date joined her in the lobby. He told her how proud he was of her for having the courage to get up and leave. They would wait together for the others. It wasn't long until couple number two joined them, and shortly couple number three came out of the theater as well. Because one young woman chose to follow the light of the Spirit inside of her, she became an example to others.

From "Recognizing and Following the Spirit," in *Living the Legacy,* 14–15.

And whoso shall receive one such
little child in my name receiveth me.

MATTHEW 18:5

THE EVAN PROJECT
DIANE M. HOFFMAN

"If every kid did something like this, just think how it could change the world." This comment was overheard at a neighborhood swimming pool last summer in Craig, Colorado, a small community of eight thousand people. It was thirteen-year-old Evan Pressley they were talking about—and still are.

Evan, a deacon in the Craig First Ward, Meeker Colorado Stake, went door-to-door in his hometown last June asking for money, not for himself, but for orphans in China. He managed to raise $2,418.45, which he turned over to a Chinese nonprofit, tax-exempt service organization headquartered near Denver, Colorado.

Evan's inspiration to help orphans living thousands of miles away in China began with his visit to that country in December of 1996. Evan accompanied his parents, Dave and Mary Pressley, when they adopted his little sister, Marianne Kai Yue. "After I got home, I just wanted to help some babies who are not as fortunate as my little sister, who has found a family." Marianne and Evan have two older brothers, Ben, nineteen, and Dan, eighteen.

As a result of traditional prejudice against females, hundreds of girls are abandoned daily in China. Evan's little sister was one of them. She had been left on a doorstep in a small village when she was only one day old. On a note attached to her clothing was the handwritten date and time of her birth: "April 15, 1996, 9:23 A.M." Eight months later, when the Pressleys took her home, she weighed only ten pounds. Poor nutrition is a fact of life for Chinese orphans. Their caregivers are very loving but lack the funds to feed the babies well.

In the spring of 1997, Evan sent a handwritten letter to Lily Nie and Joshua Zhong, directors of the agency the Pressleys had gone through to adopt Marianne, informing them of his project. His goal was to raise $2,175, and he made a list of specific things he wanted done with that money: repair a child's cleft palate and lip; buy a heavy-duty washer and dryer; provide enough formula for eight babies for one month; buy a crib and some toys; set up a small health clinic. All this for $2,175! "Money goes a long way in China," Evan explains, noting that he exceeded his goal by $243 "and 45 cents!"

In August of 1997, Evan hand-delivered the money to Lily and Joshua. And they more than honored his request. Joshua, who affectionately calls this "the Evan Project," traveled to China last fall with the money and carefully carried out Evan's itemized list. He even chose the child who would have the cleft palate surgery. The funds went to the Fusan Children's Welfare

House in Liaoning Province in northern China. "There are more than 150 children there," Evan says, "and 95 percent of them are handicapped. They'll never be adopted."

Was Evan's project easy? "A lot of people turned me down. I almost quit when I knocked on one man's door and he told me that he wouldn't contribute. He even admitted that he was hard-hearted!" Very discouraged at this point, he says, "I fasted for twenty-four hours and prayed. I told Heavenly Father that I really needed to do this, for the babies in China, and would he please help me find people who wanted to give." Evan's prayers were answered.

Several articles were published in the newspapers about the Evan Project. Later, Joshua Zhong sent a letter to one newspaper thanking the people of Craig, Colorado, for their support. He also sent a letter to Evan expressing his feelings. "I want to thank and salute you for an incredibly moving and successful fund-raising effort. I am deeply touched by your love for the Chinese children. . . . You are an amazing kid with a very BIG heart!"

Diane M. Hoffman, "The Evan Project," © by Intellectual Reserve, Inc. Previously published in the *New Era*, May 1998, 12–14.

Wherefore, be not weary in well-doing. . . . Out of
small things proceedeth that which is great.

D&C 64:33

TEMPLE TRIPS TO GO
JAMES A. SUNDBERG

Eighty-seven-year-old Rosalind Hammond proves just how vital an influence elderly members can have on others. In 1983, Rosie began to wonder how she could get to the Los Angeles Temple regularly from her home in Victorville, some one hundred miles away. She didn't drive and had no immediate family who could take her.

She prayed for inspiration and for a ride—both for herself and for others of the Victorville Stake. At one point, the stake arranged for a bus one Friday a month to encourage priesthood attendance at the temple. But the bus trips continued for only a few months.

Rosie went to her bishop with the problem. She felt prompted to ask if their ward could sponsor their own bus if she could get enough people to commit to go. The bishop agreed.

With the bishop's approval, Rosie announced the first trip, signed up all the interested people she could find, and chartered a bus. At first, it was difficult to fill it. She was so committed to the idea, however, that she paid the cost of any unfilled seats herself. "I just couldn't let the project fail," she recalls. "I want the Lord to know that there are people in Victorville who are trying hard to accomplish his work."

It took time, but finally there was a bus running to the temple consistently once a month. With phone calls and reminders and frequent expression of testimony, Sister Hammond would patiently and vigilantly fill her bus month after month.

After she had kept the bus filled for five years running, something interesting happened. Rosie's stake president called for an increase of temple attendance. He urged a 100-percent increase. Rosie wondered how she could do that. "We only got there once a month, and could do only so much while we were there," she says.

Again she felt a prompting: put together another bus trip each month. So she did. Every other Tuesday, seats fill up on Rosie Hammond's buses to the temple.

How did she do it? She first went to the regular attenders and asked for a commitment for a second trip each month. Twenty-seven people accepted the challenge. Then Rosie realized that people could go to the family history library and do research during the same hours. So she invited members and even persons who were members of other churches to join them on the trips, each for his or her own purpose.

Rosie Hammond's personal sense of urgency about the importance of work for the dead has influenced many other lives. From her own carefully kept records of the temple bus trips, for example, in one six-month period Rosie saw her companions accomplish 506 endowments, 215 sealings, 1,082 other ordinances, and 56 days of genealogical library research.

James A. Sundberg, "Rosie Hammond: Temple Trips to Go," © by Intellectual Reserve, Inc. Previously published in the *Ensign*, June 1990, 65.

MIGUEL HAD NO SHOES
ALLAN K. BURGESS AND MAX H. MOLGARD

The vital attitudes of humility and gratitude were illustrated well by a young father, Miguel, who lived in the mountains of Guatemala. He was poor in terms of worldly possessions, but rich in testimony and faith. His shirt was ragged, his pants held together with more patches than original material, and he owned no shoes. He had received little formal education, could not read or write, and he made less than three hundred dollars a year.

Miguel served as a counselor in the small Church branch in his area. The branch met in a bamboo hut that was deteriorating rapidly. The roof sagged just a little bit more each week, stark evidence that the hut would not last much longer.

The missionaries in the area were teaching a young couple who were preparing for marriage, and they were overjoyed when the couple desired to be baptized. They planned to be married and baptized the same day.

On the selected day, the couple made the long bus trip to a neighboring city. The missionaries accompanied the couple and invited Miguel to travel with them. However, the marriage and baptism took longer than expected, so the return bus had already left. They could get a ride back to the main road, but that left them with a challenging walk of seventeen miles back to the area where they lived. Because of a serious gas shortage, they knew that there was little chance of a car driving by that would give them a ride.

The couple had some relatives in the city, so they could stay. But Miguel needed to get home so he could go to work the next morning. He and the missionaries set out to walk the seventeen miles. After walking for many hours, they came to the steep two-mile climb that would finally bring them home. One of the missionaries was murmuring to himself, asking God why they had to go through this physical torture. Then he glanced over at Miguel and saw a big smile on his face. This missionary could not think of anything to smile about after fifteen miles of walking, so he asked Miguel why he was so happy. Miguel's response taught him a great lesson, for he said, "I am so happy because we just witnessed two people become members of God's true Church." The missionary looked down at Miguel's bare feet, thought of the smile that had lasted for fifteen miles, and, through Miguel, came to realize how wonderful it is to introduce the gospel to others. His fatigue and anger were replaced with gratitude and humility for the opportunity they had received of teaching and baptizing a wonderful couple.

Just a few weeks later, the devotion of Miguel was illustrated even further. The bamboo chapel had deteriorated to the point that the last meeting was being held there. During the meeting, Miguel stood up and announced that he had been secretly building another chapel for the branch and that it was completed and ready to meet in. Miguel had to work twelve hours a day, six days a week, just to earn a meager living for his family; yet he had taken nearly every penny he made and all of his extra time during the previous six months to prepare a special meeting place. He still didn't have any shoes, but he had appreciated the gospel and the members so much that he had wanted to do something special for them and for the Lord. Because of his tremendous faith and dedication, the Lord had blessed him so that the needs of his family had been taken care of.

Burgess and Molgard, *The Gospel in Action*, 117–18.

Ye yourselves will succor those that stand in need of your succor;
ye will administer of your substance unto him that standeth in need.

MOSIAH 4:16

STATISTICS OF SERVICE
LAURIE HANSEN

The following is a letter to the editor I wrote expressing my deep gratitude for the many heroes who helped my family during a time of great trial. I also sent a personal copy to many of those mentioned in the letter. The love, prayers, and service we received showed me anew that, even though it sometimes appears that we live in a discouraging time of selfishness and narcissism, there is indeed hope for today's world.

My husband was diagnosed with colon cancer eighteen months ago and died this month at the age of forty-four. I was unable to keep track of visits, phone calls, and many expressions of love. But I did write down many of the acts of kindness we received. One small act of kindness, which may seem insignificant or trivial by itself, when combined with many other such acts can mount up to immense support.

During the last eighteen months we received over 100 meals, 125 plates of treats or bakery goods, and over 500 cards or letters of good wishes. Approximately 270 people have donated money, 70 have given gifts, and over 300 people have contributed toward flowers. I kept track of at least 375 kind acts involving time or labor. The people I work with donated over 130 hours of their own vacation time so that I could have more time with Greg, giving us the greatest gift they could: time together while he was alive. People we didn't even know gave us a condominium in Hawaii for a week, and others gave us the money to finance the trip. A stay at a beach house, tickets to Disneyland, and airline tickets for our entire family, along with spending money to enjoy two full weeks in southern California were given last year so that our five daughters could enjoy their father while he still felt well. Use of a home in St. George was provided for several quick getaways. At the time Greg was diagnosed we were in the middle of building an addition on our home. Many came to help him complete the task he had started.

At times when I felt discouraged, someone would call, drop off a treat, or send just the right card. Baptists, Catholics, Episcopalians, Jews, Lutherans, Methodists, Mormons, Presbyterians, and many others offered prayers in our behalf. I figure that if every person who sent a card, meal, or treat also prayed once a day for us over the last eighteen months, it would amount to 396,575 prayers! In truth, I know there were more than five times that amount, for entire families, congregations, and prayer groups also prayed for us, many of them more than once a day.

I thank everyone from the bottom of my heart. You have pulled me through hard times and instilled in me a love for mankind for which I will be forever grateful.

"Outpouring of Love Is Inspiring." *Deseret News*, [January?] 1996.

For he that diligently seeketh shall find . . . by the
power of the Holy Ghost.

1 NEPHI 10:19

"HE HAS A LEARNING DISABILITY"
JAMES H. MCENTIRE

"Good morning, Elder. I've got a little challenge for you today." I was surprised to hear my mission president's voice on the phone. A call from the mission president was rare, to say the least.

"Elder," he continued, "I'm sending you a new missionary, a greenie." I'd been a trainer for greenies before, so I knew the president must have a special reason for calling. "His name is Elder Stanley. He's twenty-six years old, from a small town in Idaho. I'm concerned about him. He's concerned too. He has a learning disability and didn't do well in school. He finds it almost impossible to memorize. He's concerned that he won't be able to learn the discussions and scriptures. Will you make a special effort to help him?"

I said I would.

Elder Stanley arrived the next day. He wasn't a tall man—perhaps five-foot-seven inches, but he was so broad and muscular that he reminded me of the Nephites depicted in Arnold

Friberg's Book of Mormon paintings. I introduced him to the other elders in the district as my Nephite missionary companion. He beamed.

Elder Stanley had spent his life on a farm. He was a whiz at fixing mechanical equipment; he could fix any tractor, combine, pickup, or car that was put before him. More than once we would stop to help a stranded motorist. Elder Stanley would lift the hood, listen to the sound of the malfunctioning engine, and immediately pinpoint the problem. Then he'd improvise a solution, if at all possible, and send our new friend on his way. He seemed to be a genius with mechanical things.

But the discussions were another matter. Elder Stanley read slowly, stumbling over words, and he complained that he didn't do well with remembering what he'd read. He felt inadequate and uncertain. "It's been too long since I was in school," he told me. "And even then I did poorly."

"Elder, if we'll just follow the mission study program I'm confident the Lord will bless us," I said. "Maybe he'll even give us a miracle."

With that, we went to work. Or rather, Elder Stanley went to work. When we got up in the morning he would begin to study. He read the discussions during breakfast. He went over them again and again during our study time. He read them during lunch and dinner. He reviewed them at night before bedtime. I had worked with elders who studied diligently before, but not like Elder Stanley. He was determined to do all he could to qualify for the miracle he sought.

But he didn't try to do it all on his own. He prayed fervently that the Lord would help him to do what seemed impossible—to learn the missionary discussions despite his weaknesses. When he prayed with me, I could hear his humility speaking, his believing heart. He spoke to the Lord as a little child would, full of trust and confidence in the ability of his Father.

As the weeks went by, Elder Stanley blossomed in his learning ability. In fact, he soon wondered, as did I, why he had ever been worried. His diligent efforts to pay the price brought the blessing, and he seemed to learn the missionary lessons as quickly as anyone I had ever worked with. When he taught, he did so with courage and conviction, in a simple humility, and the people listened.

A lesser man might not have gone on a mission in the first place. A lesser man might have argued that twenty-six was too old to go on a mission, or that he really never could learn the discussions, or that the Lord would excuse him because of his weaknesses. Certainly there are circumstances involving physical or mental disabilities where a young man may indeed be excused from missionary service.

But Elder Stanley knew a mission was a requirement from the Lord, and he knew that if he did his part the Lord would help him. Just like Nephi—and the other Nephites—of old.

And walk in love, as Christ also hath loved us.

EPHESIANS 5:2

WHERE WERE THE STRAGGLERS?
Douglas R. Hawkes

I thought a hiking trip through the Grand Canyon would be a thrilling experience. Apparently others felt the same way. When I organized such a trip for my Boy Scouts, I ended up with thirty-five people who wanted to go, including many adults.

Most of our group arrived at the campsite, on the north rim of the canyon, the day before the hike was to take place. When the forest rangers learned that we planned to hike through to the south rim in one day, they tried to discourage us. The trail is twenty-six miles long; it starts at the north rim at about 8,000 feet and descends to 2,000 feet at the canyon floor and then back up to 6,000 feet on the south rim. It was just too much of a trek for inexperienced hikers, they said.

To make matters worse, a day or two before the hike I had injured my knee. I knew I would be unable to make the hike. Instead, I would be one of the car drivers who would meet the hikers as they came out of the canyon.

Early the next morning, we held a meeting and discussed the rangers' concerns. A few decided they wouldn't go after all; they would help transport the cars to the south rim. But most of the group were convinced they could handle the hike and were determined to go. This group included some responsible, experienced adults, and so we decided to let them go. Each person had a lunch and water. Before they left, I said to two of the adults, "Don't let anyone get behind and get separated."

Nine of us had agreed to stay behind, pack up our equipment, and then drive around to the other rim to meet the hikers that evening. It took us about three hours to clean up.

We were finally ready to leave when a familiar car appeared. In it was my twenty-two-year-old returned missionary son, Joel, who had wanted to hike but got a late start because of work. He had come down on only four hours' sleep.

Joel was a very strong and capable young man. "I think I can catch up with the others," he said, even though they had a three-hour head start. I knew enough about him to believe he could. "Watch for any stragglers," I said to him, "and help them if they need it."

He agreed, and we separated. About eight hours later, at the south rim, we began to count the hikers as they came in. The first ones came at 4:00 P.M.; others straggled in over the next three hours. By 7:00 P.M., everyone had arrived but three hikers—two young Scouts who were both very much out of shape, and my son Joel.

The evening drew on. As it grew darker we stood at the trailhead with our flashlights shining down the trail. We looked out into the vast blackness of the canyon and hollered, but we heard nothing but the whispering of the wind. We continued to wait, praying that these young men would be all right. None of the earlier group of hikers had seen them for many hours. I wondered what I would say to the mothers if their sons had met with a mishap. What if they were injured on the trail? What if one or both of them had suffered heat stroke? What if they had slipped at a dangerous point and fallen? And where in the world was Joel? My mind was sick with worry as the minutes dragged by.

Finally, we sent a "rescue party" down to look for them. They found the hikers not far from the rim, slowly making their way up.

A little after 11:00 P.M., the three hikers emerged from the darkness. They were exhausted and utterly spent, both physically and emotionally. They felt they couldn't move one more inch. But what a blessed relief that they were there!

It was later that night that I learned of the quiet heroism of my son. When he entered the canyon, he took off in a run, hoping to catch up with the rest of our group. After he had been running about two hours, he came upon these two boys, all alone and dragging. The rest of the hikers had left them, unwilling to go at the necessary snail's pace. Joel saw the condition they were in, even that early in the hike, and knew they were in trouble. They couldn't turn back—their transportation was on the south rim. They had to go on, even though it seemed impossible. Joel resolved to stay with the two slow hikers until they reached the other side, whatever it took.

The day had been extremely long and arduous, to say the least. The boys became so exhausted that they were convinced they couldn't go on. Their feet began to swell and blister. Their faces were flushed. The sun beat down on them mercilessly. At one point one of the boys fainted from exhaustion, and Joel splashed water into his face. After another long rest, they continued on.

At one point, Joel stopped with his two companions and said a heartfelt prayer with them, pleading with Heavenly Father to protect and strengthen and bless them. For hours on end he talked to them, encouraging them, motivating them to take just one more step. It grew dark, and they had no flashlight. "You can make it, guys," he said. "Just a little farther. You can do it." He thought it would never end, and they felt the same way. On and on they went. Finally, after hiking nearly eighteen hours, they emerged from the canyon. Joel had seen them through.

Instead of having the fun hike he'd hoped for, he spent those endless minutes, step after endless step, helping two utterly exhausted, discouraged young boys. With the blessings of our Heavenly Father, and with the help of their guardian and friend, Joel, they were able to conquer the impossible and return home in safety.

Stand fast in the faith, . . . be strong.

1 CORINTHIANS 16:13

"I CAN'T SING THIS"
RANDAL A. WRIGHT

While attending a youth conference in a southern state, I listened as several youth bore their testimonies. Michelle, a beautiful African-American girl, walked up to the podium and told of her life's goal to be a recording artist and of the events that had recently happened in the pursuit of this goal.

She said that she had worked hard and that it finally appeared as if her dream would come true. Representatives from a recording company came to her home with a song and offered her the opportunity to make her first recording. Michelle felt like jumping up and down, she was so excited. But then she began reading the words to the song that had been written for her, and a sick feeling came over her. She felt her newfound dream slipping away. The lyrics were not up to Church standards. They weren't too bad, but she didn't feel good about performing something that went against her values and beliefs.

There was silence in the room, and then Michelle looked up at the recording company representatives and said, "I can't sing this song. Its words go against what I believe." The people tried to convince her that one song wouldn't matter. Michelle knew what she felt, but it hurt. After all, this was the big opportunity she had been waiting for.

But some things in life cannot be bought. Michelle stood up for what she knew was right. The answer was no. She could not and would not sing that song. The representatives left, and Michelle went to her room and cried herself to sleep. But she felt good that she had had the courage to stand up for what was right.

Two days later someone knocked at Michelle's front door. There stood the same people who had visited her before. They explained that they had changed the lyrics just for her and that they still wanted her to sing it. This young woman, who stood up for what was right even when circumstances and those around her encouraged her to compromise her standards, now has her first recording out and will probably have many more to come. But more important, she knows the joy that comes from doing what is right.

From "I Can't Sing This," in *Another Ray of Sunshine for the Latter-day Saint Soul*, 222–23.

Be comforted, being knit together in love.

COLOSSIANS 2:2

"DON'T WORRY ABOUT THE STORE"
JAY A. PARRY

I was barely eighteen years old and living away from home for the first time, a student at Ricks College in eastern Idaho. It was fun to be independent and on my own. But then one day I developed a deep and nagging pain in the lower part of my abdomen. I was a typical struggling student and didn't have much money to go to a doctor. Characteristically, I went to the library with my roommate and looked in some medical encyclopedias to see if I could identify the problem. It looked like appendicitis. As the problem continued through the day, I decided I'd better get some medical help.

The doctor talked to me, examined me, did some tests and then said, "I'm afraid you have appendicitis. We're going to have to take your appendix out. And I want to do it today, before it bursts and spreads infection through your body."

I remembered an experience my father had had years before, when he was about the same age as I was. He had had appendicitis as well, and the appendix had burst, and he had nearly died. I consented to the procedure.

But first I called my parents, who lived in the Boise area. "I have appendicitis and I have to have surgery later today," I told them. I'm sure my voice was shaky. Suddenly being independent didn't seem to be so much fun.

"Is the doctor sure?"

"Yes."

"Be sure you get a priesthood blessing first."

"Okay."

"We'll be praying for you."

They told me they loved me. I told them the same. And off I went to the hospital.

The next day I was still groggy from the anesthesia and continuing doses of pain medication, and very sore. The doctor stopped in to see how I was doing. The nurses were nice. My roommates and other friends checked on me. I appreciated their concern. But without my family there I felt very much alone. Feeling weak and miserable and very far from my loved ones, I buried my face in my pillow and cried.

What I really wanted was for my parents to come and be with me. But I knew that was impossible. My dad was the owner of a grocery store and taught early-morning seminary besides. On a typical day he would arise at six in the morning, go to the church and open up the seminary room, teach the seminary students in his class (there was only one class for our entire school), go from there to the grocery store, and work from then until closing time (which was eight or nine at night, depending on the season), often without a break. He had to work so hard because he couldn't afford to hire someone to do the tasks he typically did. He worked just as hard for the Church—as a Scoutmaster, a bishop, and later in the stake presidency. If Dad ever had an evening off, it was usually because he had to attend to his Church calling.

Mom's schedule was equally demanding. She did a variety of tasks to help with the store, kept the house running smoothly, served in Church callings of her own, and was an active mother to seven children. In addition to my parents' schedules, our finances were always tight, which left little money for vacations or time off.

I really wanted my parents to be there with me. But I knew it was impossible.

I drifted in and out of sleep through most of that first day. Then in the late afternoon, I heard my mom's voice speaking to me. I thought I was dreaming. "Jay. Jay, honey, I'm sorry to wake you up, but I wanted you to know we are here."

I finally opened my eyes. There stood my mom and dad, their faces concerned but smiling.

"How could you come?" I asked.

"We had to be here with you," Dad said.

"But what about the store?"

"It's taken care of," Dad said. "Don't worry about the store."

"But you're never able to leave it. There's always so much to do."

"You're more important," Dad said. "Don't worry about the store."

I stopped worrying about the store. But I knew their sacrifice was real. They had driven nearly seven hours to get to Rexburg. The work they left undone would still have to be done when they got back home. I wasn't sure how they would ever catch up.

But they wanted to be with me when I needed them. Somehow they knew that nothing was more important to their boy lying in a distant hospital bed than to have his parents with him. And a sacrifice that sometimes seemed too great for vacations, outings, even a simple evening out—that sacrifice wasn't too great to drive all day to see their son and all day to return home several days later.

They stayed in a motel, more expense than they could afford. They spent hours with me in the hospital room. They talked to me and loved me.

It was no great act of heroism—just a simple sacrifice made by two people who loved me. But the feelings I had from those days linger, even now, thirty years later.

Even though I was trying to be independent and mature, I cried when I felt all alone and far from home in that hospital. When my parents came, unexpectedly and at great sacrifice, I wept again. Theirs was a simple act of love, offered to show their love. It was one instance of many in their lives. And I rejoice that I was able to see what they were trying to show me.

Be ye all of one mind, having compassion one
of another, . . . be pitiful, be courteous.

1 PETER 3:8

A TRUE CHAMPION
LIISA LONDON MECHAM AS TOLD TO DIANE M. HOFFMAN

A large crowd had braved snowy, treacherous weather conditions and a two-hour drive to Nephi, Utah, to cheer for our high school state championship girls' basketball game. I felt honored as I watched the townspeople troop in from our small, mountain community of Morgan, Utah. So many had come to watch us play. And boy, did they get a show! Little did I realize at that time the great lesson in life I would be taught at the end of that day.

The score teetered back and forth between the teams in that game on February 17, 1990. It was a tough game, physically and mentally. Early in the second quarter I found myself sitting on the bench, with three fouls. My position not only forced me to become an observer to the battle on the court, but also allowed me to notice the order in which the players were being substituted.

Coach, what are you doing? I thought to myself as he repeatedly put Jodi Rees, a sophomore, into the game before Trisha Garn, a junior. Trisha had been the first person off the bench all season, and now, at state, Coach Wade Fiscus was giving Trisha's time to Jodi. Jodi's abilities were certainly par, but changes like this in such an important game weren't characteristic of Coach Fiscus. I finally decided he must have a good reason and didn't question his motives.

Throughout the third and fourth quarters the game remained close. While Jodi played her best game, Trisha sat on the bench smiling and cheering her heart out for her friend. Trisha only played a few seconds of the entire championship game.

It came down to the final thirty seconds and the teams were tied. We went up by one, and then two, and finally three. A missed three-point attempt by the opposing team gave us the ball with nine seconds remaining. We were still cautious, but could taste the win. The seconds ticked down as we passed the ball to midcourt and the buzzer sounded, naming us state champions by a score of 53–50! Bedlam broke out as our fans and teammates swarmed to the floor and surrounded us. We had just achieved the goal we had worked for all year. The trophy was ours and we reveled in our moment of glory.

After the presentation of the trophies, the ladders were brought out to cut the nets down, and each team member made the climb to the top to cut a string. Finally, the net hung by one, lonely string. Hal Rees, Jodi's dad, had the honor of cutting it. He struggled awkwardly up the ladder and, gripping the scissors firmly, managed to snip the last piece.

As the net dropped to the floor tears rolled down the cheeks of our Morgan fans, and when it was placed around Mr. Rees's neck, members of the Rees family held each other tight.

I soon came to understand why Jodi had played more than Trisha. It was not because Coach Fiscus was crazy, and it was not because one player was a lot better than the other; it was because our friend and teammate had done the most unselfish thing possible—she had asked Coach to let Jodi have her playing time. Trisha Garn understood what many in the room didn't. Jodi's forty-year-old dad would not live to see her play again. He was dying of a cancerous brain tumor.

Trisha's selfless act and the sight of Hal hugging Jodi really put our state championship in perspective for me. Sure, it was nice to have the honors of men, but compared to eternal matters of family and Christlike love it didn't seem so significant.

"I don't feel like I made a sacrifice," Trisha comments. "Jodi is an outstanding athlete. I wanted to do this for my friend."

Two-and-a-half weeks after the game, Jodi's dad died. At his funeral the song "Wind beneath My Wings" was sung. Every time I hear the line from that song "Did you ever know that you were my hero?" I think of Trisha. She is my hero. And she'd probably say, "No big deal." But it's a big deal to me.

Liisa London Mecham as told to Diane M. Hoffman, "A True Champion," © by Intellectual Reserve, Inc. Previously published in the *New Era*, Mar. 1991, 12–14.

Blessed are they which do hunger and thirst after
righteousness: for they shall be filled.

MATTHEW 5:6

FILLING THE HUNGER
SHARON T. CARPENTER

I've heard it said that Church leaders are called to serve at
certain times for special reasons. This observation has come to be
very meaningful to me, in a very personal way.

For many years I had felt that there was more to be gained
from the gospel than I was experiencing. I listened to speakers say
things from the pulpit that were helpful to me, and I tried to com-
ply with every solid suggestion concerning what I could do to
enhance my spiritual progress. I paid attention in Sunday School
classes and was observant in reading scriptures and lesson man-
uals. I was diligent and temple worthy; and I accepted and willingly served in Church callings that were given me. Still I felt
weak in knowing how to fully apply the principles of the gospel
in my life—knowing how to pray more effectively, how to receive
direction from the Spirit, how to draw closer to my Father in
Heaven. It's not that I was more sinful than the next person. But
I truly wanted to be changed in my inner person. How could I
come to a change not just of behavior, but a true change of heart?

I began an intense observation of people, seeking to find someone who would understand my feelings and help me. From time to time I would venture an inquiry of someone who seemed to display the kind of life I wanted. It may have been that I didn't know the right questions to ask, but every such inquiry seemed to draw a blank. Some who knew me would answer that I was already doing well. Some would remind me of things I was already doing. But no one seemed to understand the inner longing, the intense spiritual hunger I was experiencing. This circumstance continued for a long, long while.

It wasn't that I was trying to be "truer than true," as Elder Bruce R. McConkie put it. It wasn't that I was trying to be unrealistically perfect. It wasn't that I was "looking beyond the mark." But the scriptures and the Spirit confirmed that there was indeed a "life in Christ" that was deeper and more blessed than the life I was living. And I longed to find it.

It came time for a new bishop to be called to serve our ward. The appointed Sunday came and three men were sustained as the bishopric. A few weeks after their sustaining, I began to have impressions that I should go see the new bishop. I hesitated. I knew he was busy, as all bishops are; in addition, he was just newly called and had so many things to do. But the feeling persisted: go see your bishop. I kept putting the feelings away. I didn't really have what I would call a big problem. Besides, what would I say to him?

One Sunday between meetings I somehow ended up in the hallway with the bishop. He asked me how I was doing. I said I was fine—but then blurted out my request: would he mind talking to me some day in his office? He was very gracious and said he would be glad to.

I thought perhaps in a few months, when he was more settled in his calling, we'd be able to talk. But only a very short time passed before the bishop made an appointment with me. I was fearful and shy. I didn't know how to explain my spiritual longing. I had already been disappointed on occasions before when I had tried to describe my need. Would I just be wasting his time?

The day came. I was kind of shaky as I waited in the foyer. The door opened and he invited me into his office. I sat down, and he asked what he could do for me. I told him that I didn't know what he could do, but that I would like to try to explain how I felt.

He was very patient and attentive. When I stopped talking, he paused for a moment; then he repeated back what he had heard me say, in words of his own, words that were filled with understanding and light. I started to cry. He understood! He knew how I felt!

From that day on, that bishop helped me grow. He guided my reading of scripture and other books. He listened to my questions. He understood the source of deep spiritual hunger—and knew how we can begin to be filled. He helped me to understand that true change involves a change of heart, which comes as we submit ourselves to Christ. He taught me how to "come unto Christ," so that I could more fully receive the blessings of the Atonement. Almost every talk and testimony he gave in the ward dealt with an aspect of coming unto Christ and becoming like Him. He even took time in his busy schedule to give quarterly firesides in our ward for those who chose to attend, giving additional help and inspiration. I didn't miss one. What a journey and what a joy!

It was much later that I learned that just after this brother had been called to be the bishop, but before he was sustained, he had gone to the temple, seeking to know if there was something Heavenly Father wanted him to emphasize in his service as bishop. He fasted and prayed and pleaded for an answer. After much effort, he came to a clear understanding—that at that time and in his service as bishop, he should focus on teaching the members about the life and mission of Jesus Christ. He should seek to help the members of our ward "come unto Christ," to be like Him and to be changed by Him.

I would never assume that this man was called to be the bishop just for me. Because of his inspired leadership and sacrifice many, many people were blessed—but that included me (perhaps especially me). I thank my Father in Heaven all the time for sending someone who understood the desires of my heart and was prepared and guided enough to help me begin to realize those desires. He set my foot on a path that has blessed me every day of my life.

And the Lord make you to increase
and abound in love one toward another.

1 THESSALONIANS 3:12

A CHANCE TO DANCE
DIANE M. HOFFMAN

"It all began when I said hi to Shawn in the hall one day. If you say hi once to him he's your friend. He started writing notes to me—friendly, chatty ones. Then in the spring, when I ran for student-body president, he was my greatest support."

This is how the friendship began between a shy, mentally handicapped boy and one of the most popular girls in the school.

After Mary Kay Harrop was elected student-body president of her high school in Lehi, Utah, her friendship with Shawn Broadhead continued. And he kept writing her notes. But when the time for senior prom rolled around, Mary Kay was totally clueless when Shawn's notes became hints asking her to be his date.

"The prom was not on my mind," Mary Kay says. A boy she had been dating had just left for a mission. Also she was extremely busy with her many tasks as student-body president.

One week before the prom, Shawn's father, Kent Broadhead, had business at the school and decided to talk with Mary Kay.

"I wanted to give her a way out without hurting anybody's feelings. We were assuming she wouldn't go," he said. "I explained that Shawn had been trying to ask her to the dance and he wanted to have his picture taken with her." Mary Kay's response was an unexpected but pleasant surprise. "Shawn's a great friend. I would love to go with him," she said.

"She never hesitated for a moment to accept," recalls Shawn's father.

Shawn's mother, Ladonna Broadhead, describes Shawn's reaction: "When Mary Kay called and told him she would accept his invitation, there wasn't a wall that could contain him. He called all of his friends and wrote to his brothers who were on missions. He was so excited."

The day after Mary Kay accepted Shawn's invitation, she tuned in to the Saturday morning session of April general conference. Elder Boyd K. Packer was speaking about our responsibility to the handicapped members of the Church. "When Elder Packer said we 'manifest the works of God' in our actions toward the handicapped, it hit me. I knew I was supposed to hear this talk," she says. "I realized that I was not just going to the prom to please Shawn—to do him a favor. He was doing me the favor. I was the honored one!"

Early the next week, Mary Kay was sharing her feelings with some of her friends at work. One of them made the suggestion to invite all of the special education kids to the dance. And from there, the next few days were a whirlwind. Mary Kay went to Russell Felt, the principal of Lehi High, and he gave his permission.

With the help of the special ed teacher, Dalene Callins, all the parents of the students were notified. Then Mary Kay and her mother, Alice Ann Harrop, arranged to have a turkey dinner for Shawn and nine of his classmates before the dance. "Mom did the whole meal, and my two younger sisters helped set up the tables and serve. They all really came through for us," says Mary Kay.

Rides were arranged for everyone to the hotel where the prom was being held. Mary Kay continues, "When we got there, they were all bubbling over with excitement. The sophomore class president, Jon Bailey, took turns dancing with the girls from special ed, and I danced with the boys so no one would feel left out. They were such a fun, enthusiastic group. The whole student body responded to them. One boy in a wheelchair was pulled all over the dance floor. He had the time of his life!"

Of course, Mary Kay did not forget that Shawn was her official date for the evening. "Shawn was great," she says. "He bought me the most beautiful corsage I've ever had, and he rented a tuxedo—all with money earned from a part-time job. And we did get our picture taken together."

"This experience did more for me than it did for the kids involved," claims Mary Kay. "I needed it to happen. It made the whole school year worthwhile."

So, does that mean she would do it all over again, if she could? "Absolutely! Only I'd do it sooner," she says.

Slightly modified from Diane M. Hoffman, "A Chance to Dance," © by Intellectual Reserve, Inc. Previously published in the *New Era*, Apr. 1992, 12–14.

Be kindly affectioned one to another with brotherly love.

ROMANS 12:10

"ARE YOU HAVING A BAD DAY?"
MARY ELLEN EDMUNDS

Love requires courage. To share in Christ's way is a coura-geous undertaking. Do it. Do it now. Respond to promptings that come. If we feel compassion or empathy without doing some-thing, we may diminish our power to act, to respond.

I find that I *think* of kind things more often than I *do* kind things. I'll get an idea, a prompting, but then too many times I chicken out. When I *do* respond, I have great adventures.

Once I was in a store standing in line to check out. (I have lots of experiences with that particular activity, and I almost always get in the slowest line; I don't know if it's a gift or a tal-ent.) Anyway, I noticed that the woman behind the checkout counter seemed to be in a less-than-pleasant mood. She kind of locked horns with a person ahead of me in line. I couldn't really hear or tell exactly what happened, but the clerk was not happy. A little prompting came inside of me: "Say something nice to her." "I don't want to." "She needs it." (Do you ever have con-versations like this with the still small voice?) "She'll bite my head off." Back and forth it went. I was getting closer. My heart was pounding the way it does when you sit in a testimony meeting and you know you're going to get up and you also know you're going to die at the pulpit.

And then I was there, right up close to her. She was punching the keys and all. And this is what came out of my mouth: "Are you having a bad day?" It came out kindly and gently and seemed to catch her way off guard. She looked at me, getting ready to bite, and then said, "Does it show?" "Kind of." She then told me that yes, she was having a very hard, bad, ugly day, and she told me some of the reasons why.

I didn't know what to do. I was screaming at the still small voice in my mind, "*Now* what? You didn't tell me what to do next!" But it came out: "Can I do anything to help you?" She looked at me with this what-in-the-world kind of look. It was an awkward moment. Then I said, "I know how to take out the trash." And we both laughed.

We continued talking to each other as she finished ringing up my purchases. She thanked me as I left, and I felt so happy I was grinning—not just smiling, but grinning. I felt good all over. I'm not sure if that little exchange did much for the woman at the checkout, but it made a huge difference in my day and is a sweet memory even now, years later.

Slightly modified from Edmunds, *Love Is a Verb*, 3–4.

Little children do have words given unto them many times.

ALMA 32:23

BETH'S BIRTHDAY PRESENT
Allan K. Burgess

When Beth was ten years old, her Primary teacher taught her class that Heavenly Father would answer their prayers if they asked in faith and if what they desired was right for them. Beth was the only active member of the Church in her family, and this lesson so inspired her that, upon arriving home, she immediately went to her room and began to pray. She said, "Heavenly Father, you know my father is a good man and a good father, but he never goes to church—not even when I have a part on the program. Oh, Heavenly Father, please touch my father's heart so he will want to go to church so we can become an eternal family."

Several times every day for six years Beth pleaded with the Lord in behalf of her father. Many times during these six years she would break down and cry as she poured out her soul to God. Some people may have given up after just a few months—let alone six years—but Beth's faith never faltered.

A few days before her sixteenth birthday, the family was sitting around the breakfast table. Her father asked her what she would like for her birthday. He was a well-to-do building contractor and had purchased Beth's sister a new car for her sixteenth birthday just a year before. Beth's father told her that she could have anything she wanted and that money was no problem.

Beth was about ready to suggest a new car when the Holy Ghost spoke to her and said, "Beth, here is your chance! Here is what you have been hoping and praying for all of these years!" The Spirit then told her what to ask for.

When I first heard this story I thought she was going to ask her dad to start attending church. But God had something much more powerful in mind.

After pausing a few seconds, Beth said, "Dad, there is one thing I would like to have more than anything else in this world, and it won't cost you one penny."

This really excited her father, and he wanted to know what this marvelous thing was that would not cost him anything. Beth said she would not tell him until he promised her that he would give it to her. Her father did not feel this was fair, and the rest of the family took his side, but she stood firm.

Seeing that she was not going to give in, her father finally said, "All right, I promise!"

Beth said, "Dad, the one thing I want more than anything else in this world is that we kneel down every morning together as a family in family prayer." Her father later said it was like someone dropped a ton of bricks on him—he just sat there stunned. It was a request he had least expected but knew he must fulfill in order to maintain his integrity with Beth.

The next morning, true to his word, the father called the

family together for family prayer. He called upon Beth to give the prayer because she was the only one in the family who was active. Beth gave the prayer every morning for the first week. After about a week, her mother said that she would be willing to take a turn, and it wasn't long until Beth's older sister began to pray. Soon her two little brothers were praying also. As a matter of fact, everyone in the family was praying except the father—the one who had been the focus of Beth's prayers for six years.

After about a month, as the family knelt for prayer one morning there was a pause for a moment, and then the father said, "I guess it's about my turn to pray." Beth said as her father began to pray, tears welled up in her eyes and rolled down her cheeks. She felt that she was hearing the most humble and beautiful prayer that had ever been expressed by the lips of a mortal man. It was wonderful! It was the first time she had ever heard her father pray, and the spiritual effect it had upon the whole family was overwhelming. When the prayer was over, the whole family came together in one big hug of emotion and wept in gratitude for the great blessing that had come into their home.

It wasn't long after that that the whole family began going to church together. Beth spent her seventeenth birthday in the Salt Lake Temple, kneeling at a holy altar with her family as they made eternal covenants together.

Slightly modified from Burgess, *Teach Me to Walk in the Light*, 17–19.

Bear ye one another's burdens, and so fulfil the law of Christ.

GALATIANS 6:2

WHY IS SHE HERE?
DIXIE D. ROWLEY

It was late February, and my husband, Melvin, and I decided to plow an area for our spring garden. Melvin borrowed a hand plow from one of our neighbors, and I picked out the perfect spot. I hopped on the tractor, and Melvin hooked up the plow. Just before we got to the end of the first row, the tractor jerked backward. I turned to see what had happened. Melvin was pulling on the plow; it was caught on a root. As I turned around to shut off the engine, I realized the tractor had lurched upward and was about to tip backward on me.

I fell off, twisting and landing on my stomach. In almost the same instant, the tractor came down on top of me. I remember the look of horror on Melvin's face; then I screamed as the bones in my legs were crushed into the ground. I prayed that I could stand the pain long enough to reassure Melvin I would be fine.

Hours seemed to pass before I was freed. With the help of our son Marvin and future son-in-law Tony, Melvin finally pulled me out, and they gave me a blessing. I knew I had been seriously injured, but I felt the peace of knowing my Father in Heaven was with me and would continue to give me comfort.

We didn't have a telephone, and the nearest town was an hour's drive, so it took three hours for an ambulance to arrive at our house and finally get me to the hospital. Once there, I was rushed into surgery. When I woke in my hospital room, in addition to Melvin, our Relief Society president, Sally McNabb, was standing by my bed. I remember thinking, *How did she hear about this?* and *Why is she here when she lives an hour's drive away?* But my strongest memory is the gratitude I had that she was there to help Melvin and our children. She assured me that the children would be cared for and told me not to worry about them. She spent the night at the hospital with me.

Melvin and I were relieved when the brothers and sisters in our small Arkansas branch stepped in to help with our family. Sister McNabb took our daughter Athena and our eleven-month-old Var home with her. Kay Tipton, our Young Women president, took our other five boys home with her. She lived about forty-five minutes away from our boys' school, but she drove them to and from school every day for several weeks. She took them to their Church activities, and she even brought them to the hospital to see me three or four times a week.

At first the doctors didn't think I would live. After several days they decided I would live, but they thought they might need to amputate my legs. My right leg had been crushed; my left was broken in four places. My pelvis was broken in three places. Both legs were covered with second- and third-degree burns from battery acid and gasoline that had leaked from the overturned tractor. During the next few weeks, I was in and out of surgery so often I never knew just what was going on.

One thing I did know—there was always someone there for me. The Relief Society arranged for the sisters in our branch to take turns covering three shifts a day at the hospital so someone would be with me twenty-four hours a day. They kept this up for the first six weeks, then stayed about ten hours a day for the next six weeks. I know these sisters had families; many of them also had health problems. Yet they regularly made the sacrifice to travel many miles to be with me.

The sisters also fasted and prayed for me. They served willingly and gave me strength when I was too weak to face each day alone. I was in the hospital for three months and was still in a full body cast for another three months after I returned home. All this time the sisters continued to serve me and my family. I was witnessing what Alma spoke of—"having [our] hearts knit together in unity and in love one towards another" (Mosiah 18:21).

The doctors were able to save my legs but doubted I would ever walk again. I believe it was because of their good care, combined with the faith of my family and priesthood holders and Relief Society sisters, that I am alive today and able to walk again. These wonderful heroes saved me from a life as an invalid—and changed my perspective on Christlike service forever.

Slightly modified from Dixie D. Rowley, "It Took a Tragedy," © by Intellectual Reserve, Inc. Previously published in the *Ensign*, Mar. 2000, 62.

Now at this time your abundance may be a supply for their want.

2 CORINTHIANS 8:14

GIVING STREET CHILDREN A CHANCE
JAN U. PINBOROUGH

The twenty-five children who are learning to read and write on Lubian Sequi's patio are poor—too poor to afford shoes or uniforms or supplies for school. Some have no beds at home, sleeping instead in cardboard boxes on the ground.

Lubian Sequi is a small, lovely woman with a smile that warms and comforts. On the chalkboard she has written the words *Dios Me Ama* ("God Loves Me"). Besides teaching her students reading, writing, mathematics, social studies, and etiquette, Sister Sequi begins each day's classes with a prayer and a lesson from the Bible. She also encourages the children to pray with their families. She provides pencils, notebooks, and chalk for the children who cannot afford them, and she uses many visual aids to help the children learn.

This unusual teacher finds most of her students on the streets of Santo Domingo, in the Dominican Republic. "Whenever I see a dirty, barefoot, or neglected child, I say to him, 'Come here. Don't be afraid. Where do you live?'" Then she goes home with the child to ask permission for the child to attend school in her home.

Once a month, she invites the parents to an evening meeting where they can see how the children are progressing. She also gives a talk to help the parents spiritually and morally. "Our intention is to teach the parents so they can teach their children better," she says. Although it is not Sister Sequi's primary goal to convert, at least one student's family has been baptized since coming to her school.

With a college degree in elementary education, Sister Sequi taught in the public schools for twenty-four years. She was also a nurse and a social worker. "I have always had a great attraction to the poor," she says, "and in spite of my imperfections I have tried to help them." When she was younger, she sometimes went to the countryside on a donkey, taking clothes to the people and preaching the gospel.

Her experience as a nurse also affected her deeply. "In the hospitals, I learned to love a lot, because there is a lot of love and pain there. Each time I had to take care of a patient, I would ask myself, 'If he were Jesus, how would I care for him?' With this idea in mind, I learned to love the sick without fear, nausea, or grief and to see in each person the image of the Lord."

In 1961 Lubian Sequi founded a vocational school to teach young women skills that could help them live a better life. She still administers this school, where more than three hundred students learn sewing, tailoring, pastry-making, weaving, and other manual skills. The school is supported by a nominal tuition, which varies according to the students' ability to pay.

Lubian and her husband, Felix, joined the Church in 1980, eight years after they married. They discovered the gospel at a welfare fair held by the sister missionaries. "I was first attracted to the Church by its concern with helping families and also by its philosophy that the gospel is to be taken to everyone," she recalls. Since then she has served as Relief Society president, and Brother Sequi now serves as the director for the Church Educational System in the Dominican Republic. The Sequis have a son, Gustavo Adolfo, fifteen, and a daughter, Nadia, who is twelve. Nadia often helps Sister Sequi in her work.

Sister Sequi's greatest desire is to spend her strength working—first for her family and then in behalf of others. "My goal is not to build a house in this life, because nothing is permanent here," she explains. "I want to build our house in heaven because we will be there forever."

If you were to ask Sister Sequi's young students what kind of house their teacher is building in heaven, they would say it is a very big one indeed—with room enough for all those she has come to love.

Jan Underwood Pinborough, "Lubian Sequi: Giving Street Children a Chance," © by Intellectual Reserve, Inc. Previously published in the *Ensign*, Feb. 1988, 61–62.

*But there is a spirit in man: and the inspiration of the
Almighty giveth them understanding.*

JOB 32:8

———✦———

THE RIGHT THING AT THE RIGHT TIME
CLARK STIRLING REES

Sometimes a person can change another's course in life
simply by saying the right thing at the right time. The trick (or
the spiritual gift!) is to know what to say and when to say it.

When my wife, Allison, was young, she was a very conscien-
tious and serious girl. She was also quiet and proper, sensitive and
very nice looking. She attracted lots of boys and always had dates.
And it seemed that there were always additional boys waiting in
line.

One summer she began to date a returned missionary, James
Turner. He began to monopolize her time, and soon the other
fellows got pushed out of the way. James and I had been friends
for a long time. I watched as their relationship developed. One
night we were all at a dance. During the intermission James and I
were alone. He pulled a small box out of his pocket and showed
me an engagement ring. I wasn't surprised.

She accepted his proposal. A week or so later, Allison
attended a Turner family gathering to celebrate the engagement.

One of James's aunts and his mother came forward with two wine glasses, complete with wine, and proposed that the newly engaged couple toast one another. James reached for one glass and waited for Allison to lift the other. She didn't do it. The family members began to murmur. "Come on, Allison," James's mother said. "It's only a toast."

"I'm sorry," Allison said. "I don't feel comfortable doing it."

Soon thereafter James took her home. It was a long and uncomfortable ride.

That was Allison's first clue that not all was right with James and his commitment to Church principles. There were other clues as well. She began to become unsure and doubtful about the pending marriage. She was fearful of what she might be getting herself into.

One Sunday, right after Sunday School, she decided to walk through the cultural hall to be alone. She needed some time to think. She had been there only a moment when her Sunday School teacher came in. "I could tell something was wrong today, Allison," he said. "What is it?" She hesitated, but finally told him what was troubling her. That was when he said exactly the right thing at the right time. In fact, it was so perfect we believe he must have been guided by the Spirit. "If you can think of any man you would rather be married to, then don't go through with your marriage to James."

She could think of such a man. She didn't consider him a real possibility, but she knew her Sunday School teacher was right. If there was someone else who seemed like a better choice, she should cancel her engagement to James. A few days later, in the church parking lot after a meeting, she returned the ring.

That night I was in the foyer of that same meetinghouse, having just put away the materials I had used for a Scout meeting. I noticed a group of young ladies talking excitedly. I went over to see what all the commotion was about. There in the middle of the group was Allison. She was flushed and trembling. "What's the matter?" I quietly asked, speaking to one of Allison's friends. "What happened to Allison?"

"She just broke off her engagement to James," she said.

A little later, when Allison was mostly alone, I went over to her and said, "Would you like to go out Friday night?"

She was completely surprised. "You must just be feeling sorry for me," she said. I insisted I wasn't, and we went on the date. One thing led to another—we eventually married in the temple and have had a wonderful life together.

Allison has said on many occasions how thankful she is for that Sunday School teacher. It was really a simple thing he did. But by being in tune enough to follow her into the cultural hall, by being in tune enough to say precisely the right thing to help her open her heart to what the Spirit wanted to tell her, he was able to change the entire course of her life.

Oh, and the man Allison thought of that day in the cultural hall, the man she'd rather marry than James? Who would have imagined it would be me!

Charity never faileth.

1 CORINTHIANS 13:8

HE DIDN'T EVEN RECOGNIZE HIM
NAME WITHHELD BY REQUEST

Last summer Brother Jacobs, an elderly temple worker, had a stroke and was taken to the hospital. My father was his home teacher and visited him often. He also checked in on Sister Jacobs weekly.

After several weeks, Brother Jacobs was progressing nicely and seemed to be doing quite well. Then suddenly, without warning, he had another stroke that left him paralyzed.

Dad continued to visit Brother Jacobs, but the elderly man's condition grew steadily worse. Soon he had lost his memory and had no idea who was in the room with him. Still my dad continued his visits.

Gangrene now set in, and Brother Jacobs lost his leg. Then he began to lose his sight. There he lay in his hospital bed, slowly dying. The orderlies did not enjoy feeding or shaving him, for he was not a pleasant sight. So, before Sister Jacobs would come to visit her beloved husband, my father would go into the room and shave the old man's face.

For weeks this routine continued; the weeks became months,

and still the old man clung to life. He could recognize no one, he had no idea what was going on around him, and yet he continued to live.

One Sunday after church, my father asked our family if we could wait while he stopped at the hospital on our way home. It was a hot and muggy day, but we agreed if Dad promised not to take too long.

Later, on our way home, I asked Dad if Brother Jacobs had recognized him.

"No," was his reply, "I don't think so."

Throughout the next week I wondered why Dad would continue to visit a person who did not even know he was there. What difference could Dad's visits possibly make?

One week later Brother Jacobs passed away, and my father was given the task of dressing his body for the funeral. At the viewing, Brother Jacobs looked so peaceful. As my father stood beside the casket of the man he had been assigned to love, I finally realized that his caring was true charity, the pure love of Christ.

From Yorgason and Yorgason, *Becoming*, 111–12.

Cast thy bread upon the waters:
for thou shalt find it after many days.

ECCLESIASTES 11:1

———————

"DAD, HERE'S ALL MY MONEY"
PETER A. WILSON

My Grandma and Grandpa Wilson were never wealthy. They lived in a modest but comfortable home in the San Francisco Bay area. Grandpa spent most of his life as a sheet-metal worker. Grandma stayed home with their four children. They were active in the Church and raised their children to be the same—but Grandpa struggled with a tobacco habit he'd picked up as a young teenager. He was able to quit for awhile from time to time—sometimes for months at a time—but then in a time of stress the habit would reassert itself and he'd start smoking again.

Grandpa Wilson was a good man with a good heart. It seemed he was always looking for ways to bless other people. And he was kind and thoughtful to Grandma. He was ashamed of his secret habit—his bishop knew, of course, but he was able to hide it from most ward members—and he wanted his children to be better than he was.

Their youngest child was a son named Ron, after Grandpa. Ron was a bright and studious child. He applied himself to his studies, and it was apparent that he would go far academically. But after high school he decided to delay his college studies. Instead, he went to work. He was thrifty in his use of his money and saved most of what he earned, after tithing. When he was of age to go on a mission, he made application and received a call to serve in France. He was delighted.

Using his own money, he purchased all his clothes, his shoes, and other necessities. "I don't want to be a burden on you," he told his mom and dad.

At that time, a missionary's monthly payments weren't paid to the ward; instead, money was sent directly to the missionary, who paid all his bills directly. Ron made arrangements with the bank to transfer all his money to an account in his dad's name. Then he said, "Dad, here's all my money. I've saved enough for my entire mission, so you and Mom won't have to sacrifice for me. All you'll need to do is send me the monthly check I need, and I'll do just fine."

Ron left for his mission as scheduled. Every month the check came, signed with his Dad's name, just as Ron had arranged. It gave him a great deal of satisfaction to know that he had earned his own way on his mission. He worked hard, learned the language, taught the people, lived the rules, wrote home faithfully. It was a hard experience but very rewarding.

Finally it was time to go home. As Ron traveled home, he reviewed his plan for the next year or two. He would go back to work and save as much as he could. He would continue to be frugal. Then he would finally be able to proceed with the college education he so much desired.

On Ron's first night home his dad gave him his bank account book. "There was a little left over," Grandpa said. "Maybe you can use it to get started on your schooling."

Ron opened the book. There was the entire amount he had saved for his mission—thousands of dollars, plus interest. Not one penny had been spent. He was astounded. "What happened? Why is all the money still here?"

"Mama and I wanted you to have a head start on your education when you got back," Grandpa said. "Besides, why should you get all the blessings from your mission? We decided we could sacrifice and support you while you served the Lord. And He provided the way for us to do it."

Ron did proceed with his college education. He earned a bachelor's degree, a master's, and finally a Ph.D. With his "mission money" he was able to move much more quickly through his years of schooling, with much less debt than he had anticipated. He received full blessings of paying for his own mission, Grandma and Grandpa received full blessings for paying for Ron's mission, and Ron was able to go to school—all on the "same" money!

Let every man esteem his brother as himself.

D&C 38:24

HE CARRIED ME IN HIS ARMS
CHAD BOWMAN

It sounded like a great outing—three-wheeling in the desert. Even though I wasn't a 100-percent church attender, my Young Men leaders wanted me to go with them to the sand dunes and have some fun. One of my best friends, Brent, who also was not a 100-percenter, decided to go along and take his own three-wheeler.

The dunes looked good to us. We unloaded and off we went on my friend's vehicle. He even let me drive—but only for a little while. "What's the matter, Chad? You're going so slow! Why are you such a chicken!" He soon took over the driving privileges.

Late in the day Brent said he was going to show me what a real jump felt like. With the two of us riding high, he headed for a small hill. What we didn't see was that the other side had a big drop off, and we were soon flying through the air, having left the three-wheeler behind. All I remember is the feeling of air beneath me and the impression of darkness all around me. And then massive pain. I awoke to the sound of motors. I looked around and saw nothing but sand. I realized that no one could see me where I was and that one of those "motors" could run right over me. With all of my might, somehow I struggled over a fence and fell once more into the sand and blacked out again. I thought I would die.

The next thing I remember was the voice of one of my leaders talking to me. It was Jerry. I don't know how he found me. "Where does it hurt?" he asked. I told him I hurt all over. "Can you get up? Can you walk?" I tried, but I could hardly move. Jerry was slender, of average height, but strong. He didn't outweigh me by very much. But, surprisingly, he picked me up and started to walk. He carried me all the way back to camp, tromping over the sand for over a mile, carrying me in his arms. It was hot and sweaty work. We were both very thirsty, without any water on us. Not once did he complain about the burden. Instead, he tried to encourage me. "You're going to be all right, Chad. Don't worry, we'll get you taken care of." I needed the encouragement. I was in great pain, and I wondered if I would survive.

As we continued on that long and terrible hike, I couldn't believe that Jerry could walk so far carrying me. Something must have strengthened him physically and spiritually, so that he could help me in my need. He didn't falter even once.

Finally we arrived back at camp, where two of the other leaders were waiting. "What happened?" they asked. "Let's take a look. Oh, I don't think he's hurt too badly." When I complained of the intense pain in my shoulder, they said that my shoulder was probably just "out." One of the men said he knew how to pop shoulders back in. "I've done it several times." He told me to get up on the picnic table. "I'll fix it for you." *No! No!* I thought. I felt helpless and scared inside.

Jerry sensed my fear and shook his head. "No way," he said, wedging himself between me and the man. "I'm going to take him to the hospital." The men weren't being cold or insensitive—they just thought they knew how to help. But Jerry stood up for me even though he was the youngest leader there.

He loaded me into his car, and the two of us went to a hospital. We were so far out in the desert that the drive took several hours. The emergency room doctor did an examination and took some X-rays. "You have severe fractures of your collarbone," he said. "No wonder you're hurting so much." They did what they could to stabilize me; then Jerry took me home to my parents so I could get the additional care I needed.

It's hard to comprehend how Jerry could have made such a sacrifice for me. Going out to find me when it seemed I was missing. Carrying me for a mile or more across rough terrain, without complaint. Sticking up for what was best for me, even in contradiction to older and more experienced leaders. Giving up most of an outing that he himself had been looking forward to, in order to bless and help me. Jerry showed uncommon courage and strength both physically and spiritually. I will always be thankful for his amazing, inspired help.

By their desires and their works you shall know them.

D&C 18:38

THE MAN AT THE GAS STATION
KIRKHAM PARRY

Last July I was traveling back from Arizona to our home in Provo, Utah. In the early evening we stopped at a gas station in southern Utah to get gas. I waited in the car with my brothers and sister while my dad got out to fill the car with gas. My mom went into the gas station.

Feeling bored and tired, I watched the other people gassing up their cars. My window was tinted so they couldn't see me. One man stood out from the others. He looked to be about thirty (exactly twice my age). Judging from his appearance, I guessed he was probably a Mormon. He truly stood out. He wasn't the most handsome man in the world. He drove an old, run-down car, wore inexpensive clothes, and had ragged, beat-up shoes. But that wasn't what drew my attention.

He had a little son who was "helping" him pump the gas. In every interaction with his son I could see the greatest love and patience. I could see it in his face, his gestures, his touch. I could see how attentive he was to the things his little boy was saying. He seemed to be demonstrating, by his actions, that there was nothing else in the entire world, at that moment, that was more important than his son was to him. He didn't know anyone was watching him. I knew I was seeing him as he really was, not as he wanted others to think he was. He was the genuine article—a great father to a little boy.

When he went in to pay for his gas I thought he looked a bit discouraged. He may have been worried about his lack of money. But I also thought, judging from what I'd seen of his relationship with his son, that he must feel that with his family he had all he really needed. And I thought how that was right—it wouldn't matter if I was the poorest person in the world, as long as I had my family.

My total exposure to that man couldn't have lasted more than five minutes. If I saw him today I probably wouldn't recognize him. But I'm certain I will remember him to the day I die.

I'd like to thank this brother for his unspoken, unknowing Christlike example. He truly changed my life by just being there, loving and gentle, patient and kind, to an energetic son. Often when I get discouraged I think of that man, and he helps me go on with a much improved attitude.

Be [ye] followers of that which is good.

1 PETER 3:13

"WE WANT TO BE YOUR FRIENDS"
MIRIAM PARKER

For many children, recess is the best part of the school day. My nine-year-old son (I'll call him Eric) had a group of friends that would gather every recess break and have a great time together.

But as the year progressed, many members of Eric's group began to use offensive language. They began to try out swear words as they played.

This was very troublesome to Eric. He didn't swear and never wanted to. In fact, he was worried enough about it that he talked to me and his dad, asking what he should do. He wondered if he should stop playing with those friends.

"It's hard to be around that kind of thing, Eric," we agreed. "Even if you're not participating yourself, it doesn't feel good to hear it, does it." He agreed; that's exactly how he felt. We talked about tolerance and acceptance of those who are different and how we should love them anyway.

But we refrained from telling him what to do. "Sometimes

only one person can make a difference in a group," we said. "We want you to be prayerful and do what you think is right."

He made his decision and went to school. During recess when the other kids began to swear, Eric asked them in as nice a way as he could to please not use that kind of language around him.

They laughed. "That's dumb," they said. "What's wrong with those words? Besides, we can't help it—the words just come out of our mouths."

Eric was hurt and disappointed, but he continued to play with the group at recess time. He thought maybe he could help them.

Then one day at recess, a swear word slipped out of Eric's mouth so quickly that he was shocked. He knew it had been an accident, but he felt sick about it. What if it happened again? What if it got worse? Again he wondered what to do.

The next day he told his friends that since they wouldn't stop swearing, he wouldn't play with them anymore. After that he began to find other friends. Sometimes he spent the entire recess by himself. It made him feel sad, because the children he had played with for so long really were his friends, and they were lots of fun to be with. But he didn't want to hear their swearing, and he didn't want to slip again. He resolved that it was better to find new friends, or to be alone, than to swear.

Time went by; recesses came and went.

One day Eric noticed two members of his old group running toward him at recess. He got kind of afraid and wondered if he should run the other way. Were they going to try to hurt him? He chose to stay where he was.

He was nervous as they drew closer. But still he waited.

When they reached where he was, one of the kids said, "Eric, we want to be your friends. If we stop swearing, will you come and play with us again?"

Eric's answer was a relieved "yes." That was two years ago. Now Eric and his friends are closer than ever. And not one of them uses bad language when they play.

Some have compassion, making a difference.

JUDE 1:22

THE OTHER GIRL BEGAN TO CRY
Sheri Lynn Dorrance

One year the young women from our ward qualified to compete in the regional basketball tournament. Tensions were high. We were undefeated that year, but it was our first time at regionals and we were nervous. We had worked hard and we showed up ready to play hard. Many ward members were there to support us.

The game seemed to turn into a fight almost as soon as it began. Our opponents were aggressive and pushy. One of the other team's players was acting particularly tough and mean; in the process, she offended our entire team, especially the girl on our team who was assigned to guard her.

Then parents from our ward began to join in the negative spirit. They began to complain loudly. They yelled at the referee. They talked about how unfair the game was; they argued that the other team shouldn't be allowed to be so rude.

Then our coaches started to join in the criticisms as well.

The whole evening deteriorated quickly. Just about everyone on the two teams was snapping at everyone else on the opposing side. Many plays broke down into arguments. By the time the game was over, everyone from our ward was highly upset. We had lost badly, and everyone was angry at the other team and its rowdy players. As our team gathered into a little group at the end of the game, we were all bitter and tired. We had no desire to go congratulate our opponents for the win, as we usually did. The adults from our ward agreed with us. "Let's just get out of here," one mother said.

As we all turned to leave, Tina, one of the players from our ward, started to walk across the gym floor toward the other team. We watched, surprised. What was she doing?

Tina headed straight for the player on the other team who had been the most offensive. When Tina reached her, she put her arms around the "enemy," gave her a warm, heartfelt hug, and said, "Good game. I'm sorry for the way my team acted. Good luck in your next game." The recipient of the hug began to cry.

We were all stunned. We knew in our hearts that what Tina had done was courageous and right. At the same time, we knew the negative, angry feelings we were harboring in our hearts. We felt chastened and humbled.

A few weeks later, our Young Women president gave a lesson on charity in our Young Women meeting. And at the end of her lesson, she asked Tina to stand. "Tina, these flowers are for you," she said, handing her a large and beautiful bouquet. "We want to thank you for being such a good example at our regional basketball game. You made the hard choice and set an example for us all—including the adults."

A few years have passed since that game, but members of the

ward still remember it. They remember how rough and hard it was. And they remember the quiet hero who walked alone across the gym floor to do the right thing.

I am with thee to save thee and to deliver thee, saith the Lord.

JEREMIAH 15:20

FINDING MATTHEW
FRED AND JENNIE JANZEN

Jennie: In 1978, we went on a family camping trip to the high Uintas (mountains in northeastern Utah) over the twenty-fourth of July weekend. The camping spot we chose was at Butterfly Lake. With Fred and me were Steve (age 18), Matthew (age 7), and our twins, Brian and Darin (age 6). Two other sons, David and Wayne, were elsewhere on that particular weekend.

It was so cold on that first night that we decided in the morning to pack up and go home. But first we wanted to take a short hike down to Scutter Lake, only a mile away, to see some of the beautiful Utah scenery. On the way back, Fred and I stopped to tie the shoelace of one of our twins. Steve was a little way ahead of us. When Matthew kept going, Fred and I assumed he would catch up with Steve.

When we reached the top of the trail, we saw Steve standing alone by the car. "Where is Matthew?" we asked. Steve answered that he hadn't seen him. Suddenly we were filled with great fear and panic. Fred quickly searched one trail while Steve searched another. When Steve came back alone, I told him to stay with the twins and I ran back down the trail calling Matthew's name over and over. I asked other hikers if they had seen a seven-year-old boy wearing a red tank top shirt and blue jeans. No one had. I don't have the words to describe the terrible feelings that filled my soul on that dreadful, dark day. How could I live without this wonderful little boy? Father in Heaven, please help me to find him, I prayed, pleading constantly for his help.

When I met Fred on the trail, we knelt together and pleaded with the Lord to help us find our child—and, until we found him, to comfort him and keep him safe. The forest service was contacted and other hikers, hearing of our plight, joined the search. Still he was not found.

Hours passed. I made a bed for Brian and Darin in the back of our station wagon and stayed with them as they slept. Steve and Fred continued the search. Gradually my fears increased and my heart sank into overwhelming grief. I have always thought I was a woman of faith. But in my despair, I couldn't understand why my prayers weren't being answered. I had faith, but still my child wasn't found.

At sundown, the forest service said it was too dangerous to search in the dark. Fred said that we would go home to get more help. He took the flashlight and walked the Mirror Lake trail one more time. When the flashlight and Fred again appeared alone, I felt my heart breaking.

We got in our car and started home. Fred tried to comfort me, telling me that he had given Matthew a father's blessing from afar, and that the Spirit had whispered that our son was all right.

Fred didn't know if this meant he was dead or alive, but he knew Matthew wasn't suffering or hurting. As we drove home in silence, I felt every turn of the wheel as we drove farther and farther down the mountain—farther and farther from my child. I was so sad and frightened. How could I possibly leave my precious little boy all alone in the dark of the mountains? There were times when I felt I could hardly breathe. When we finally arrived home, I ran into Matthew's room and fell on my knees sobbing and pleading again with my Lord for help.

Around midnight, I called our bishop. I also called Dick Veenendaal, a friend who was a member of the Green Berets with expertise in searching for and finding people lost in the wilderness. I changed into some night clothes, but I couldn't lie down or sleep. I kept pacing all night.

Then our heroes began to come.

Dick arrived with some helpers, and Fred left with them for the Uintas. Bishop Don Nelson arrived. He said he had called our stake president, Ben Banks. Through priesthood channels, phone call after phone call was made, not just in our ward but throughout the stake. Sleepy men got out of their beds to help in the mountain search. Eileen Ragsdale, our Relief Society president, arrived at our house at the same time as the bishop. As the three of us knelt in prayer, Bishop Nelson felt impressed to promise me that Matthew would be found and he would be safe. A feeling of peace came over me.

By about 3:30 A.M., thirty to forty men from our ward had gathered at our ward meetinghouse for prayer. Shortly later, many additional men from the stake responded to the call. One of them, Kerry Jacobson, a newly returned missionary, had a broken foot in a cast. Yet he had the feeling he should help in the search. His father, one of the bishops in the stake, suggested he take his motorbike since he couldn't walk.

The next day, one of the sisters in our ward, Helen Morris, offered to organize the sisters to make sack lunches for the searchers. When she was buying the luncheon meat at Charlie's Market, the butcher asked her why she was buying so much. When she told him what it was for, he took the package back, and wrote "no charge." He said he would just like to help.

In the night, two of my neighbors, Ann Kessler and Linda Larsen, came to give me encouragement and comfort. They stayed the entire night. By morning my doorbell began to ring. Friends and neighbors came to tell me they were praying for us. When Brian and Darin woke up, Ann took them home with her for the day.

We also contacted extended family members. Some were able to join in the search. We all prayed and fasted that day. Everyone was so worried.

Fred: By 9:00 A.M. of the second day, I was thoroughly exhausted. I had hiked all the previous day looking for Matthew, had been up all night, and continued to hike into the morning. When I ran into Bishop Nelson and a group of priesthood brethren from the ward, I was so overwhelmed I fell upon the bishop's shoulders and began to sob. I sat down on a rock, overcome with emotion. As the men passed, they tried to console me. I continued back up the trail and after a few minutes saw President Banks with more priesthood brethren coming down the trail. I sat down and sobbed again. I felt as I did when I was a little boy at the movies, watching the cavalry ride to the rescue.

After about an hour, I came to the top of the trail and noticed a young man on a motorbike starting down the trail. This was a restricted area, where motor vehicles were not allowed. I got upset at him and said to myself, "How can you help me find Matthew? You can't go into the primitive area with a bike." (I would later come to regret my anger. We need to sometimes not be so quick to judge.)

As time passed, additional people began to hear about the lost child and came to help. In the end there were some 350 people searching for Matthew. But as the morning wore on, I became more discouraged. After awhile, I felt the need to earnestly pour out my soul to the Lord. I walked a short distance away to a quiet meadow and knelt down by a large rock. There I prayed for a miracle—to have Matthew walk out of the woods. But miracles do not always come when we want them.

Jennie: At about 1:00 P.M., a ward friend, Phyllis Jensen, felt impressed to comfort me by reading from the book *Faith Precedes the Miracle*, by President Spencer W. Kimball. She knew my eyes would be red and puffy from crying, and that I wouldn't be able to read myself. The bishop's counselor, Dean Baxter, and his wife,

Lauramay, who had just returned from being out of town, also came to see if they could help.

Fred: I became more distraught and discouraged and felt the need to pray for the Lord's help. I walked over to the meadow where I had been before and began to plead with the Lord in the depths of humility. (While previously I thought I was humble, this time I *really* became humble.) After a few minutes, I returned to find some men with horse trailers pulling into the area. It was a neighbor and some of his friends who belonged to the Ute Rangers—more cavalry. Our neighbor said he was prepared to stay until Matthew was found. (A few months earlier Jennie had helped his bedridden wife by bringing meals to his family for two weeks, and he had been very impressed by her kindness.)

With cars and trucks and horse trailers arriving, we began to get some congestion on the road. I walked onto the road to help direct traffic. As I did, I saw that same young man riding past on a motorbike, this time with a dirty little kid on the back. At first I didn't take much notice of them. But when I looked again, I saw it was Matthew! I grabbed him in my arms and held him tight, while I said to the same motorcyclist I had been angry with earlier, "Oh, how I love you!" I learned later that the young man's name was Kerry Jacobson, a recently returned missionary who had felt impressed to help even though he had broken his foot and was wearing a cast.

As I held Matthew, his first words were, "I prayed five times."

Jennie: A few minutes after 1:00 P.M. the phone rang. It was the dispatcher in the Duchesne County Sheriff's Office. Matthew was found! He was a little dehydrated but other than that he was all right. I began to cry and fell to my knees, thanking my Heavenly Father for this miracle. Phyllis Jensen, the Baxters, and I knelt in prayer, and Dean offered a prayer of thanksgiving for the safe return of Matthew.

When Matthew arrived home, I took him in my arms, hugging and kissing him. My joy was complete. When I calmed down enough to let him talk, he told me he had prayed five times and that he knew if he stayed on the trail he would be all right.

Matthew had been missing about twenty-seven hours. Through His love, our Father in Heaven had watched over our boy and helped him to be safe and to be comforted. And through an army of loving friends and neighbors, a miracle occurred—not just in finding Matthew, but in our hearts. We felt the love of God, we felt the selfless love of both friends and strangers, and we knew we would never be the same again.

And if it so be that you should labor all your days . . . and bring,
save it be one soul unto me, how great shall be your joy
with him in the kingdom of my Father!

D&C 18:16

THERAS QUATHEL ALLRED
NADA ALLRED MIDKIFF

My father, Theras Quathel Allred, was a man as unusual as his name. Through a long life of extraordinary service, he taught me the true meaning of charity, of the importance of watching over the widow and the afflicted.

Dad often played a game to make service fun. One game was to shovel our elderly neighbor's walks before they could get out and do it themselves. When it snowed, we would see Dad standing by our bay window chuckling and smiling—for the game was about to begin! Not long after, he would deploy the forces up and down the block to begin shoveling snow. One sister told me that he continued to shovel her walk long into his eighties. Even then he would never have quit of his own accord. His body had to give out first.

One of Dad's best lessons on love came through his service to the widow Blanche Young.

Blanche Young was supremely frightening to an eight-year-old girl. She was the most mysterious, cantankerous person I ever met as a child. All the neighbors in the area seemed to keep their distance—few really knew her or even seemed to want to. For many decades she had been inactive in the Church, and she wanted absolutely no contact with the ward. She was now extremely old.

I remember walking past Sister Young's house one day after school. I was with a large group of children, and to stay with the group I walked across her grass. Sister Young came running out onto her front porch and gave me a good scolding for not staying on the sidewalk. Later that day, with an immensely self-righteous attitude, I told my father what happened and firmly declared, "I hope I never see her again! She scares me!" It was then my father gently informed me that Sister Young had a child who had been killed while on a mission. This tragedy had been too much for her to bear. He asked me to be more patient and kind in my judgment of others.

Years later my father was in charge of home teaching in the ward. He promptly assigned himself the five hardest families—all were less active and wanted nothing to do with the Church. I was surprised to see that Blanche Young was on the list. Within days my father left our home to make his first visit. My old childhood fears rose in my heart, and I anxiously waited for him to return home. I feared it wouldn't go very well.

Dad walked to her home, told her that he would like to be her home teacher, and explained to her exactly what a home teacher does. "Sister Young, can I have your permission to come and visit you on a regular basis?"

She minced no words. "Theras, I never wanted any home teachers and don't plan on starting now—so don't come by again."

Dad was prepared for that response and said, "Now, Sister Young, you are getting to be elderly, and it is dangerous for you not to have someone check on you every once in awhile to make sure you're all right. Can I at least stop by to see if you are okay?"

She grudgingly agreed, probably thinking that my father wouldn't follow through very well, as had been the case with others in the past. But she didn't know my dad.

Once a month he began to visit Sister Young's home to see if she was okay. But that was only the excuse; of course, he really went to serve her. He shoveled her walks, raked her leaves, and delivered goodies my mother had baked. He bought her groceries and took her to the store. This continued for years. From time to time Dad would ask if he could come in and give her a home teaching message. The answer was always the same, "I don't want a home teacher!"

One summer my dad noticed that all her bushes were overgrown. "Would you like me to prune your shrubs?" he asked.

"I would love it," she replied. "It would sure help if you could also cut down that tree in my backyard. I'll pay you for your work."

The tree was huge—about 2 ½ stories high. By this time Dad was in his late seventies—but he was as excited as a kid to be able to serve Sister Young in this way. He and a fellow ward member, Brother Tom Bullock, worked together to trim the bushes and shrubs. Then he and and Brother Bullock spent several weeks cutting the tree down, chopping it up for firewood, and stacking it.

As Dad was finishing the final clean-up, Sister Young came out on her front porch with her checkbook. "How much do I owe you?" she asked.

"Sister Young," Dad replied, "I am your home teacher. I don't do these things for pay. I do them because I love you."

Sister Young wouldn't accept that. "I don't feel good about this," she said. "You've spent weeks on that tree. It was hard work. Now, Theras, you've got to let me pay you something."

"All right," Dad said, "I'll tell you how you can repay me. Would you allow me to come into your home once a month and give you a message?"

After all the years of love and service, capped by Dad's hard work on the tree, Sister Young felt truly loved and appreciated as a neighbor. She couldn't say no. She allowed him to start teaching her the gospel. But she still refused to attend church.

The Lord truly loved this good woman, and He once again set up a situation to help her. After Dad had been teaching her for quite some time, one day she mentioned that she was having some problems with the wiring in her home. I'm sure Dad's eyes lit up at the opportunity. He said, "Oh, I can take care of that!" He spent a whole Saturday working on the electrical problems.

When he was finished, once again Sister Young got out her checkbook. She said, "Theras, you used some of your own money buying electrical supplies. You've spent a whole day doing the work. I need to pay you for this!"

Father answered gently, "Sister Young, I am your home teacher. I don't do these things for pay. I do them because I love you."

"No, I insist," she said. "You can't just do all this for free. I need to pay you."

"All right," Dad replied. "If you really want to pay me something, let me have the privilege of taking you to church this Sunday."

Sister Young couldn't refuse. She knew Dad loved her. After decades of complete inactivity, she attended church that Sunday and consistently thereafter. Dad continued to serve her until she died. Through his example she became one of my favorite neighbors. (Incidentally, he served as diligently at the homes of all the other families he home taught—and every single one of those families returned to Church activity.)

I can hear what my Dad would say if he were reading this today: "Now, Nada, I was the one who was blessed through my little efforts, far more than anyone else." And, of course, he would be right. He was filled with a light and a joy in the Spirit that came from a lifelong effort to give of himself to others. He truly learned the truth of the Savior's words, "For whosoever will save his life shall lose it; and whosoever will lose his life for my sake shall find it" (Matthew 16:25).

BOOKS CITED

Another Ray of Sunshine for the Latter-day Saint Soul. Salt Lake City: Bookcraft, 1999.

Burgess, Allan K. *Becoming a Celestial Person in a Telestial World.* Salt Lake City: Bookcraft, 1990.

————. *Teach Me to Walk in the Light.* Salt Lake City: Bookcraft, 1995.

Burgess, Allan K., and Max H. Molgard, *The Gospel in Action.* Salt Lake City: Bookcraft, 1992.

Canfield, Anita R. *A Perfect Brightness of Hope.* Salt Lake City: Deseret Book, 1991.

Edmunds, Mary Ellen. *Love Is a Verb.* Salt Lake City: Deseret Book, 1995.

Grassli, Michaelene, Dean Packer, and Steve Woodhead, comps. *Dad, You're the Best!* Bookcraft, 1994.

High Fives and High Hopes. Salt Lake City: Deseret Book, 1990.

Living the Legacy. Salt Lake City: Deseret Book, 1996.

Lynn, Wayne R. *Lessons from Life: Inspiring Insights from the School We All Attend.* Salt Lake City: Bookcraft, 1987.

Peterson, H. Burke. *A Glimpse of Glory.* Salt Lake City: Bookcraft, 1986.

Wright, Randal A., comp. *Why Say No When the World Says Yes? Resisting Temptation in an Immoral World.* Salt Lake City: Deseret Book, 1993.

Yorgason, Blaine M., and Brenton G. Yorgason, *Becoming.* Salt Lake City: Deseret Book, 1986.

―――. *Others.* Salt Lake City: Bookcraft, 1978.

SCRIPTURE INDEX

INDEX

ABOUT THE AUTHOR

Jay A. Parry has worked as an editor for the *Ensign* magazine, as a freelance writer, and as an editor for Deseret Book Company.

Brother Parry has served in The Church of Jesus Christ of Latter-day Saints as a bishop, a high councilor, and as chair of a general Church curriculum writing committee.

A prolific writer, he has most recently published *Everyday Miracles: True Stories about God's Hand in Our Lives.* With Donald W. Parry as coauthor, he has published *Understanding the Signs of the Times; Understanding the Book of Revelation;* and *Understanding Isaiah.* He is also one of the creators and compilers of the successful "Best-Loved" series, which includes *Best-Loved Stories of the LDS People* (three volumes), *Best-Loved Poems of the LDS People, Best-Loved Humor of the LDS People,* and *Best-Loved Talks of the LDS People.*

He and his wife, Vicki Hughes Parry, are the parents of seven children and have four granddaughters.